T0283421

Web Development and Design

Web Development and Design

Carson Thomas

Larsen & Keller
www.larsen-keller.com

Web Development and Design
Carson Thomas
ISBN: 978-1-64172-076-2 (Hardback)

© 2019 Larsen & Keller

 Larsen & Keller

Published by Larsen and Keller Education,
5 Penn Plaza,
19th Floor,
New York, NY 10001, USA

Cataloging-in-Publication Data

Web development and design / Carson Thomas.
    p. cm.
Includes bibliographical references and index.
ISBN 978-1-64172-076-2
1. Web site development. 2. Web sites--Design. I. Thomas, Carson.
TK5105.888 .W43 2019
006.76--dc23

For more information regarding Larsen and Keller Education and its products, please visit the publisher's website www.larsen-keller.com

Table of Contents

Permissions

Index

Preface

The work involved in developing a website for the Internet or intranet is known as web development. Some of the tasks inherent to web development include web engineering, web design, content development, web server configuration, network security configuration, etc. Development of innovative tools and technologies has resulted in dynamic and interactive websites. Allowing an interaction between applications and users, error checking, preventing frauds and protecting sensitive information are important concerns in web development. Web design refers to the processes involved in the production and maintenance of websites. It includes interface design, web graphic design, user experience design, search engine optimization, etc. This book unfolds the innovative aspects of web development and web design, which will be crucial for the holistic understanding of the subject matter. The topics included in this book are of the utmost significance and bound to provide incredible insights to the readers. It will serve as a reference to professionals and students engaged in these fields.

A short introduction to every chapter is written below to provide an overview of the content of the book:

Chapter 1, Internet can be defined as a global system of computer networks which uses the internet protocol suite to connect devices across the world. The diverse applications and importance of internet and World Wide Web in the modern day world have been thoroughly discussed in this chapter; **Chapter 2** The development of a website for the internet or the intranet is termed as web development. The diverse aspects of web development such as website, web server, web engineering, web design, etc. have been thoroughly discussed in this chapter. **Chapter 3**, The use of different skills and disciplines for the production and maintenance of a website is called web design. This chapter has been carefully written to provide an easy understanding of the varied facets of web design such as user experience design, user interface design, flash, motion graphics, etc.; **Chapter 4**, Web programming is the creation of dynamic web applications, for e-commerce sites, social networking sites, etc. The field of web programming has seen improved dynamic and interactive websites, due to an ever-growing set of technologies and tools. This chapter discusses in detail about asm.js, HTML5 audio, Opa, etc.; **Chapter 5**, The web architecture is a software framework which is designed with the aim of supporting the development of applications for the web, such as web resources, web services and web APIs. The topics addressed in this chapter on web browser, HTML, URL, HTTP, etc. will provide an extensive understanding of web architecture; **Chapter 6**, The process of buying or selling or making any transaction online falls under the wide spectrum of e-commerce. The diverse aspects of e-commerce such as billing settlement plan, digital currency, electronic trading, etc. have been thoroughly discussed in this chapter.

I extend my sincere thanks to the publisher for considering me worthy of this task. Finally, I thank my family for being a source of support and help.

Carson Thomas

An Introduction to the Internet

Internet can be defined as a global system of computer networks which uses the internet protocol suite to connect devices across the world. The diverse applications and importance of internet and World Wide Web in the modern day world have been thoroughly discussed in this chapter.

The Internet is a global system of interconnected computer networks that use the standard Internet protocol suite (TCP/ IP) to serve billions of users worldwide. It is a network of networks that consists of millions of private, public, academic, business, and government networks, of local to global scope, that are linked by a broad array of electronic, wireless and optical networking technologies. The Internet carries a vast range of information resources and services, such as the interlinked hypertext documents of the World Wide Web (WWW) and the infrastructure to support electronic mail.

In the present age of information technology, use of Internet is becoming quite popular for accessing information on any topic of your interest. It also provides tremendous opportunities to students, researchers and professionals for getting information on matters related to academic and professional topics and lot more.

For the students and educational purposes the internet is widely used to gather information so as to do the research or add to the knowledge of various subjects. Even the business professionals and the professionals like doctors, access the internet to filter the necessary information for their use. The internet is therefore the largest encyclopedia for everyone, in all age categories. The internet has served to be more useful in maintaining contacts with friends and relatives who live abroad permanently.

Working of Internet

While the working of internet can get as complex as one can expect, making it similar to other day to day activities eases out the understanding process by quite a lot. Let us suppose that every house in our locality is equivalent to a device that uses internet, such as a smart phone or a tablet computer. The addresses that the houses have are just similar to the IP address, which is unique and unavailable for any other device all around the world. The posts and phone calls that arrive in the house are sources through which the world connects to the house and through the same medium the people in the houses communicate with the outside world. Writing down the mails or picking the phone instrument to make is quite similar to connecting to the internet or rather opening a web browser.

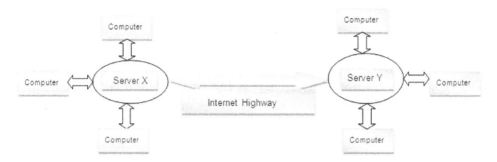

Figure: Block Diagram Explaining Basic Internet Operation

To send and receive the posts or phone calls, exchange offices and post offices are there which are just similar to the servers that store all the data and make it dynamically available. The calls we make are first directed to the telephone exchange office that checks whether the number we have dialled is valid or not. It is quite similar to the protocols that are applied when user requests for data exchange. Just as the number of houses decide a place to be called as village, town, city or state; number of internet connected devices define an area to be categorized into LAN, MAN, WAN etc.

Figure: Image of Google Search Engine Home Page

Interacting with various internet based services is fairly graphical interfaces which nowadays entertain the surfers with quality interactive multimedia content. The web pages are programmed in such a way so that the from highest quality videos to multi lingual texts, everything is available to the users.

Services of Internet -E-mail, FTP, Telnet

Email, discussion groups, long-distance computing, and file transfers are some of the important services provided by the Internet. Email is the fastest means of communication. With email one can also send software and certain forms of compressed digital image as an attachment. News groups or discussion groups facilitate Internet user to join for various kinds of debate, discussion and news sharing. Long-distance computing was an original inspiration for development of ARPANET and does still provide a very useful service on Internet. Programmers can maintain accounts on distant, powerful computers and execute programs. File transfer service allows Internet users to access remote machines and retrieve programs, data or text.

E-Mail

E-mail or Electronic mail is a paperless method of sending messages, notes or letters from one person to another or even many people at the same time via Internet. E-mail is very fast compared to the normal post. E-mail messages usually take only few seconds to arrive at their destination. One can send messages anytime of the day or night, and, it will get delivered immediately. You need not to wait for the post office to open and you don't have to get worried about holidays. It works 24 hours a day and seven days a week. What's more, the copy of the message you have sent will be available whenever you want to look at it even in the middle of the night. You have the privilege of sending something extra such as a file, graphics, images etc. along with your e-mail. The biggest advantage of using email is that it is cheap, especially when sending messages to other states or countries and at the same time it can be delivered to a number of people around the world.

It allows you to compose note, get the address of the recipient and send it. Once the mail is received and read, it can be forwarded or replied. One can even store it for later use, or delete. In e-mail even the sender can request for delivery receipt and read receipt from the recipient.

(i) Features of E-mail:

- One-to-one or one-to-many communications

- Instant communications

- Physical presence of recipient is not required

- Most inexpensive mail services, 24-hours a day and seven days a week

- Encourages informal communications

(i) Components of an E-mail Address

As in the case of normal mail system, e-mail is also based upon the concept of a recipient address. The email address provides all of the information required to get a message to the recipient from anywhere in the world. Consider the e-mail ID.

In the above example john is the username of the person who will be sending/

receiving the email. (john@hotmail.com) Hotmail is the mail server where the username john has been registered and com is the type of organization on the internet which is hosting the mail server.

FTP (File Transfer Protocol)

File Transfer Protocol, is an internet utility software used to uploaded and download files. It gives access to directories or folders on remote computers and allows software, data and text files to be transferred between different kinds of computers. FTP works on the basis of same principle as that of Client/ Server. FTP "Client" is a program running on your computer that enables you to communicate with remote computers. The FTP client takes FTP command and sends these as requests for information from the remote computer known as FTP servers. To access remote FTP server it is required, but not necessary to have an account in the FTP server. When the FTP client gets connected, FTP server asks for the identification in terms of User Login name and password of the FTP client. If one does not have an account in the remote FTP server, still he can connect to the server using anonymous login.

Using anonymous login anyone can login in to a FTP server and can access public archives; anywhere in the world, without having an account. One can easily Login to the FTP site with the username anonymous and e-mail address as password.

(i) Objectives of FTP :

   • Provide flexibility and promote sharing of computer programs, files and data

   • Transfer data reliably and more efficiently over network

   • Encourage implicit or indirect use of remote computers using Internet

   • Shield a user from variations in storage systems among hosts.

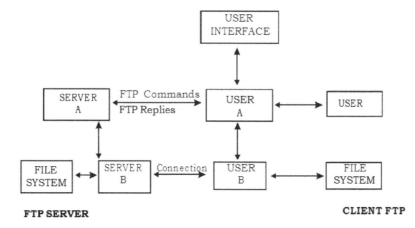

(ii) The basic steps in an FTP session

- Start up your FTP client, by typing ftp on your system's command line/'C>' prompt (or, if you are in a Windows, double-click on the FTP icon).

- Give the FTP client an address to connect. This is the FTP server address to which the FTP client will get connected λ Identify yourself to the FTP remote site by giving the Login Name

- Give the remote site a password

- Remote site will verify the Login Name/Password to allow the FTP client to access its files

- Look directory for files in FTP server

- Change Directories if required λ Set the transfer mode (optional);

- Get the file(s) you want, and

- Quit.

Telnet (Remote Computing)

Telnet or remote computing is telecommunication utility software, which uses available telecommunication facility and allows you to become a user on a remote computer. Once you gain access to remote computer, you can use it for the intended purpose. The TELNET works in a very step by step procedure. The commands typed on the client computer are sent to the local internet service provider (ISP), and then from the ISP to the remote computer that you have gained access. Most of the ISP provides facility to Telnet into your own account from another city and check your e-mail while you are travelling or away on business.

The following steps are required for a TELNET session

- Start up the TELNET program

- Give the TELNET program an address to connect (some really nifty TELNET packages allow you to combine steps 1 and 2 into one simple step)

- Make a note of what the "escape character" is

- Log in to the remote computer,

- Set the "terminal emulation"

- Play around on the remote computer, and

- Quit.

Types of internet connections

There are five types of internet connections which are as follows:

    (i)   Dial up Connection

    (ii) Leased Connection

    (iii) DSL connection

    (iv) Cable Modem Connection

    (v) VSAT

Dial up connection

Dial-up refers to an Internet connection that is established using a modem. The modem connects the computer to standard phone lines, which serve as the data transfer medium. When a user initiates a dial-up connection, the modem dials a phone number of an Internet Service Provider (ISP) that is designated to receive dial-up calls. The ISP then establishes the connection, which usually takes about ten seconds and is accompanied by several beepings and a buzzing sound.

After the dial-up connection has been established, it is active until the user disconnects from the ISP. Typically, this is done by selecting the "Disconnect" option using the ISP's software or a modem utility program. However, if a dial-up connection is interrupted by an incoming phone call or someone picking up a phone in the house, the service may also be disconnected.

Advantages

- Low Price
- Secure connection – your IP address continually changes
- Offered in rural areas – you need a phone line

Disadvantages

- Slow speed.
- Phone line is required.
- Busy signals for friends and family members.

Leased Connection

Leased connection is a permanent telephone connection between two points set up by a telecommunications common carrier. Typically, leased lines are used by businesses to connect geographically distant offices. Unlike normal dial-up connections, a leased line is always active. The fee for the connection is a fixed monthly rate. The primary factors affecting the monthly fee are distance between end points and the speed of the circuit. Because the connection doesn't carry anybody else's communications, the carrier can assure a given level of quality.

For example, a T-1 channel is a type of leased line that provides a maximum transmission speed of 1.544 Mbps. You can divide the connection into different lines for data and voice communication or use the channel for one high speed data circuit. Dividing the connection is called multiplexing.

Increasingly, leased lines are being used by companies, and even individuals, for Internet access because they afford faster data transfer rates and are cost-effective if the internet is used heavily.

Advantage

- Secure and private: Dedicated exclusively to the customer

- Speed: Symmetrical and direct

- Reliable: Minimum down time

- Wide choice of speeds: Bandwidth on demand, easily upgradeable

- Leased lines are suitable for in-house office web hosting

Disadvantages

- Leased lines can be expensive to install and rent.

- Not suitable for single or home workers

- Lead times can be as long as 65 working days

- Distance dependent to nearest POP

- Leased lines have traditionally been the more expensive access option. A Service Level Agreement (SLA) confirms an ISP's contractual requirement in ensuring the service is maintained. This is often lacking in cheaper alternatives.

DSL Connection

Digital Subscriber Line (DSL) is a family of technologies that provides digital data transmission over the wires of a local telephone network. DSL originally stood for digital subscriber loop. In telecommunications marketing, the term DSL is widely understood to mean Asymmetric Digital Subscriber Line (ADSL), the most commonly installed DSL technology. DSL service is delivered simultaneously with wired telephone service on the same telephone line. This is possible because DSL uses higher frequency bands for data separated by filtering. On the customer premises, a DSL filter on each outlet removes the high frequency interference, to enable simultaneous use of the telephone and data.

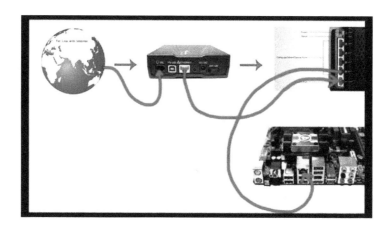

The data bit rate of consumer DSL services typically ranges from 256 kbit/s to 40 Mbit/s in the direction to the customer (downstream), depending on DSL technology, line conditions, and service-level implementation. In ADSL, the data throughput in the upstream direction, (the direction to the service provider) is lower, hence the designation of asymmetric service. In Symmetric Digital Subscriber Line (SDSL) services, the downstream and upstream data rates are equal.

Advantages:

- Security: Unlike cable modems, each subscriber can be configured so that it will not be on the same network. In some cable modem networks, other computers on the cable modem network are left visibly vulnerable and are easily susceptible to break in as well as data destruction.

- Integration: DSL will easily interface with ATM and WAN technology.

- High bandwidth

- Cheap line charges from the phone company.

- Good for "bursty" traffic patterns

Disadvantages

- No current standardization: A person moving from one area to another might find that their DSL modem is just another paperweight. Customers may have to buy new equipment to simply change ISPs.

- Expensive: Most customers are not willing to spend more than $20 to $25 per month for Internet access. Current installation costs, including the modem, can be as high as $750. Prices should come down within 1-3 years. As with all computer technology, being first usually means an emptier wallet.

- Distance Dependence: The farther you live from the DSLAM (DSL Access Multiplexer), the lower the data rate. The longest run lengths are 18,000 feet, or a little over 3 miles.

Cable Modem Connection

A cable modem is a type of Network Bridge and modem that provides bi-directional data communication via radio frequency channels on a HFC and RFoG infrastructure. Cable modems are primarily used to deliver broadband Internet access in the form of cable Internet, taking advantage of the high bandwidth of a HFC and RFoG network. They are commonly deployed in Australia, Europe, Asia and Americas.

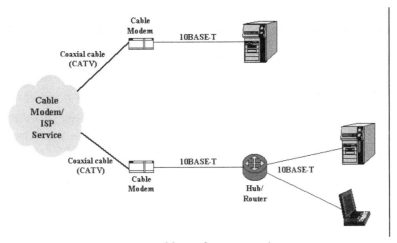

Figure: Cable modem connection

Figure above shows the most common network connection topologies when using cable modems. The cable TV company runs a coaxial cable into the building to deliver their Internet service. Although fed from the same coax that provides cable TV service, most companies place a splitter outside of the building and runs two cables in, rather than using a splitter at the set-top box. The coax terminates at the cable modem.

The cable modem itself attaches to the SOHO computing equipment via its 10BASE-T port. In most circumstances, the cable modem attaches directly to a user's computer. If a LAN is present on the premises (something many cable companies frown upon), some sort of router can be connected to the cable modem.

Advantages

- Always Connected: A cable modem connection is always connected to the Internet. This is advantageous because you do not have to wait for your computer to "log on" to the Internet; however, this also has the disadvantage of making your computer more vulnerable to hackers. Broadband: Cable modems transmit and receive data as digital packets, meaning they provide high-speed Internet access. This makes cable modem connections much faster than traditional dial-up connections.

- Bandwidth: Cable modems have the potential to receive data from their cable provider at speeds greater than 30 megabits per second; unfortunately, this speed is rarely ever realized. Cable lines are shared by all of the cable modem users in a given area; thus, the connection speed varies depending upon the number of other people using the Internet and the amount of data they are receiving or transmitting.

- File Transfer Capabilities: Downloads may be faster, but uploads are typically slower. Since the same lines are used to transmit data to and from the modem, priority is often given to data traveling in one direction.

- Signal Integrity: Cable Internet can be transmitted long distances with little signal degradation. This means the quality of the Internet signal is not significantly decreased by the distance of the modem from the cable provider.

- Routing: Cable routers allow multiple computers to be hooked up to one cable modem, allowing several devices to be directly connected through a single modem. Wireless routers can also be attached to your cable modem.

- Rely on Existing Connections: Cable modems connect directly to preinstalled cable lines. This is advantageous because you do not need to have other services, such as telephone or Internet, in order to receive Internet through your cable modem. The disadvantage is that you cannot have cable internet in areas where there are no cable lines.

Disadvantages

- Cable internet technology excels at maintaining signal strength over distance. Once it is delivered to a region, however, such as a neighborhood, it is split among that regions subscribers. While increased capacity has diminished the effect somewhat, it is still possible that users will see significantly lower speeds at peak times when more people are using the shared connection.

- Bandwidth equals money, so cable's advantage in throughput comes with a price. Even in plans of similar speeds compared with DSL, customers spend more per Mb with cable than they do with DSL.

- It's hard to imagine, but there are still pockets of the United States without adequate cable television service. There are far fewer such pockets without residential land-line service meaning cable internet is on balance less accessible in remote areas.

VSAT

Short for Very Small Aperture Terminal, an earthbound station used in satellite communications of data, voice and video signals, excluding broadcast television. A VSAT consists of two parts, a transceiver that is placed outdoors in direct line of sight to the satellite and a device that is placed indoors to interface the transceiver with the end user's communications device, such as a PC. The transceiver receives or sends a signal to a satellite transponder in the sky. The satellite sends and receives signals from a ground station computer that acts as a hub for the system. Each end user is interconnected with the hub station via the satellite, forming a star topology. The hub controls the entire operation of the network. For one end user to communicate with another, each transmission has to first go to the hub station that then retransmits it via the satellite to the other end user's VSAT.

Advantages

Satellite communication systems have some advantages that can be exploited for the provision of connectivity. These are:

- Costs Insensitive to Distance
- Single Platform service delivery (one-stop-shop)
- Flexibility
- Upgradeable
- Low incremental costs per unit

Disadvantages

However like all systems there are disadvantages also. Some of these are

- High start-up costs (hubs and basic elements must be in place before the services can be provided)
- Higher than normal risk profiles
- Severe regulatory restrictions imposed by countries that prevent VSAT networks and solutions from reaching critical mass and therefore profitability
- Some service quality limitations such the high signal delays (latency)
- Natural availability limits that cannot be mitigated against
- Lack of skills required in the developing world to design, install and maintain satellite communication systems adequately

Downloading Files

File downloading is the process of copying a file (such as a game or utility) from one computer to another across the internet. When you download a game from our web site, it means you are copying it from the author or publisher's web server to your own computer. This allows you to install and use the program on your own machine.

Here's how to download a file using Internet Explorer and Windows XP. (This example shows a download of the file "dweepsetup.exe" from Dexterity Games.) If you're using a different browser such as Netscape Navigator or a different version of Windows, your screen may look a little different, but the same basic steps should work.

1. Click on the download link for the program you want to download. Many sites offer multiple download links to the same program, and you only need to choose one of these links.

2. You may be asked if you want to save the file or run it from its current location. If you are asked this question, select "Save." If not, don't worry — some browsers will automatically choose "Save" for you.

3. You will then be asked to select the folder where you want to save the program or file, using a standard "Save As" dialog box. Pay attention to which folder you select before clicking the "Save" button. It may help you to create a folder like "C:\Download" for all of your downloads, but you can use any folder you'd like.

4. The download will now begin. Your web browser will keep you updated on the progress of the download by showing a progress bar that fills up as you download. You will also be reminded where you're saving the file. The file will be saved as "C:\Download\dweepsetup.exe" in the picture below.

   Note: You may also see a check box labeled "Close this dialog box when download completes." If you see this check box, it helps to uncheck this box. You don't have to, but if you do, it will be easier to find the file after you download it.

5. Depending on which file you're downloading and how fast your connection is, it may take anywhere from a few seconds to a few minutes to download. When your download is finished, if you left the "Close this dialog box when download completes" option unchecked, you'll see a dialog box as shown in figure below:

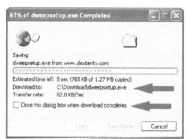

Downloading window

6. Now click the "Open" button to run the file you just downloaded. If you don't see the "Download complete" dialog box, open the folder where you saved the file and double-click on the icon for the file there.

What happens next will depend on the type of file you downloaded. The files you'll download most often will end in one of two extensions. (An extension is the last few letters of the filename, after the period.) They are:

*   .EXE files: The file you downloaded is a program. Follow the on-screen instructions from there to install the program to your computer and to learn how to run the program after it's installed.

*   .ZIP files: ZIP is a common file format used to compress and combine files to make them download more quickly. Some versions of Windows (XP and sometimes ME) can read ZIP files without extra software. Otherwise, you will need an unzipping program to read these ZIP files. Common unzipping programs are WinZip, PKZIP, and Bit Zipper, but there are also many others. Many unzipping programs are shareware, which means you will need to purchase them if you use them beyond their specified trial period.

Advantages of Internet

*   E-mail: Email is now an essential communication tools in business. With e-mail you can send and receive instant electronic messages, which works like writing letters. Your messages are delivered instantly to people anywhere in the world, unlike traditional mail that takes a lot of time. Email is free, fast and very cheap when compared to telephone, fax and postal services.

*   24 hours a day - 7 days a week: Internet is available, 24x7 days for usage.

*   Information: Information is probably the biggest advantage internet is offering. There is a huge amount of information available on the internet for just about every subject, ranging from government law and services, trade fairs and conferences, market information, new ideas and technical support. You can almost find any type of data on almost any kind of subject that you are looking for by using search engines like google, yahoo, msn, etc.

    ◦   Online Chat: You can access many 'chat rooms' on the web that can be used to meet new people, make new friends, as well as to stay in touch with old friends. You can chat in MSN and yahoo websites.

    ◦   Services: Many services are provided on the internet like net banking, job searching, purchasing tickets, hotel reservations, guidance services on array of topics engulfing every aspect of life.

    ◦   Communities: Communities of all types have sprung up on the internet. Its a great way to meet up with people of similar interest and discuss common issues.

○ E-commerce: Along with getting information on the Internet, you can also shop online. There are many online stores and sites that can be used to look for products as well as buy them using your credit card. You do not need to leave your house and can do all your shopping from the convenience of your home. It has got a real amazing and wide range of products from household needs, electronics to entertainment.

○ Entertainment: Internet provides facility to access wide range of Audio/ Video songs, plays films. Many of which can be downloaded. One such popular website is YouTube.

○ Software Downloads: You can freely download innumerable, softwares like utilities, games, music, videos, movies, etc from the Internet.

Limitations of Internet

- Theft of Personal information: Electronic messages sent over the Internet can be easily snooped and tracked, revealing who is talking to whom and what they are talking about. If you use the Internet, your personal information such as your name, address, credit card, bank details and other information can be accessed by unauthorized persons. If you use a credit card or internet banking for online shopping, then your details can also be 'stolen'.

- Negative effects on family communication: It is generally observed that due to more time spent on internet, there is a decrease in communication and feeling of togetherness among the family members.

- Internet addiction: There is some controversy over whether it is possible to actually be addicted to the Internet or not. Some researchers claim that it is simply people trying to escape their problems in an online world.

- Children using the Internet has become a big concern. Most parents do not realize the dangers involved when their children log onto the Internet. When children talk to others online, they do not realize they could actually be talking to a harmful person. Moreover, pornography is also a very serious issue concerning the Internet, especially when it comes to young children. There are thousands of pornographic sites on the internet that can be easily found and can be a detriment to letting children use the Internet.

- Virus threat: Today, not only are humans getting viruses, but computers are also. Computers are mainly getting these viruses from the Internet. Virus is is a program which disrupts the normal functioning of your computer systems. Computers attached to internet are more prone to virus attacks and they can end up into crashing your whole hard disk.

- Spamming: It is often viewed as the act of sending unsolicited email. This multiple or vast emailing is often compared to mass junk mailings. It needlessly

obstruct the entire system. Most spam is commercial advertising, often for du-
bious products, get-rich-quick schemes, or quasi-legal services. Spam costs the
sender very little to send — most of the costs are paid for by the recipient or the
carriers rather than by the sender.

World Wide Web

WWW stands for World Wide Web. A technical definition of the World Wide Web is :
all the resources and users on the Internet that are using the Hypertext Transfer Protocol (HTTP).

A broader definition comes from the organization that Web inventor Tim Berners-Lee
helped found, the World Wide Web Consortium (W3C).

The World Wide Web is the universe of network-accessible information, an embodi-
ment of human knowledge.

In simple terms, The World Wide Web is a way of exchanging information between
computers on the Internet, tying them together into a vast collection of interactive multimedia resources.

Internet and Web is not the same thing: Web uses internet to pass over the information.

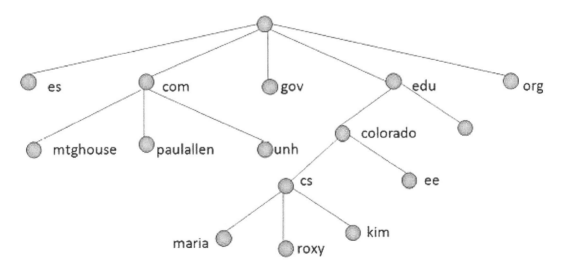

World Wide Web was created by Timothy Berners Lee in 1989 at CERN in Geneva.
World Wide Web came into existence as a proposal by him, to allow researchers to
work together effectively and efficiently at CERN. Eventually it became World Wide
Web.

The following diagram briefly defines evolution of World Wide Web:

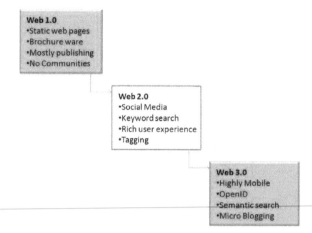

WWW Architecture

WWW architecture is divided into several layers as shown in the following diagram:

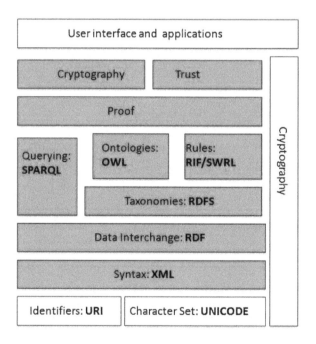

Identifiers and Character Set

Uniform Resource Identifier (URI) is used to uniquely identify resources on the web and UNICODE makes it possible to build web pages that can be read and write in human languages.

Syntax

XML (Extensible Markup Language) helps to define common syntax in semantic web.

Data Interchange

Resource Description Framework (RDF) framework helps in defining core representation of data for web. RDF represents data about resource in graph form.

Taxonomies

RDF Schema (RDFS) allows more standardized description of taxonomies and other ontological constructs.

Ontologies

Web Ontology Language (OWL) offers more constructs over RDFS. It comes in following three versions:

- OWL Lite for taxonomies and simple constraints.

- OWL DL for full description logic support.

- OWL for more syntactic freedom of RDF

Rules

RIF and SWRL offers rules beyond the constructs that are available from RDFs and OWL. Simple Protocol and RDF Query Language (SPARQL) is SQL like language used for querying RDF data and OWL Ontologies.

Proof

All semantic and rules that are executed at layers below Proof and their result will be used to prove deductions.

Cryptography

Cryptography means such as digital signature for verification of the origin of sources is used.

User Interface and Applications

On the top of layer User interface and Applications layer is built for user interaction.

WWW Operation

WWW works on client- server approach. Following steps explains how the web works:

1. User enters the URL (say, http://www.tutorialspoint.com) of the web page in the address bar of web browser.

2. Then browser requests the Domain Name Server for the IP address corresponding to www.tutorialspoint.com.

3. After receiving IP address, browser sends the request for web page to the web server using HTTP protocol which specifies the way the browser and web server communicates.

4. Then web server receives request using HTTP protocol and checks its search for the requested web page. If found it returns it back to the web browser and close the HTTP connection.

5. Now the web browser receives the web page, It interprets it and display the contents of web page in web browser's window.

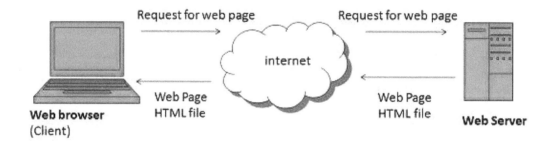

Future

There had been a rapid development in field of web. It has its impact in almost every area such as education, research, technology, commerce, marketing etc. So the future of web is almost unpredictable.

Apart from huge development in field of WWW, there are also some technical issues that W3 consortium has to cope up with.

User Interface

Work on higher quality presentation of 3-D information is under deveopment. The W3 Consortium is also looking forward to enhance the web to full fill requirements of global communities which would include all regional languages and writing systems.

Technology

Work on privacy and security is under way. This would include hiding information, accounting, access control, integrity and risk management.

Architecture

There has been huge growth in field of web which may lead to overload the internet and degrade its performance. Hence more better protocol are required to be developed.

2

Web Development

The development of a website for the internet or the intranet is termed as web development. The diverse aspects of web development such as website, web server, web engineering, web design, etc. have been thoroughly discussed in this chapter.

Web development refers to building, creating, and an maintaining websites. It includes aspects such as web design, web publishing, web programming, and database management.

While the terms "web developer" and "web designer" are often used synonymously, they do not mean the same thing. Technically, a web designer only designs website interfaces using HTML and CSS. A web developer may be involved in designing a website, but may also write web scripts in languages such as PHP and ASP. Additionally, a web developer may help maintain and update a database used by a dynamic website.

Web development includes many types of web content creation. Some examples include hand coding web pages in a text editor, building a website in a program like Dreamweaver, and updating a blog via a blogging website. In recent years, content management systems like WordPress, Drupal, and Joomla have also become popular means of web development. These tools make it easy for anyone to create and edit their own website using a web-based interface.

While there are several methods of creating websites, there is often a trade-off between simplicity and customization. Therefore, most large businesses do not use content management systems, but instead have a dedicated Web development team that designs and maintains the company's website(s). Small organizations and individuals are more likely to choose a solution like WordPress that provides a basic website template and simplified editing tools.

JavaScript programming is a type of web development that is generally not considered part of web design. However, a web designer may reference JavaScript libraries like jQuery to incorporate dynamic elements into a site's design.

Components of Website

While every website is built slightly differently, there are a few fundamental components that handle every interaction between a user and the site:

- Client: The local computer (desktop/laptop) or device (phone/tablet) the user is interacting with to access the website.

- Server: The remote computer that "physically houses" all the files (and thus code) that make up the website.

- Database: A sub-component of the remote server, the database is a large series of data tables used to store all the dynamic information generated or used within the website. For example, the account information of a logged in user would be stored in the database.

With our three fundamental components identified, we can briefly examine how a website recognizes a visiting user and ultimately displays the appropriate page for viewing. The following diagram provides an approximate illustration of the process.

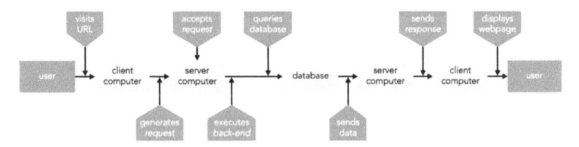

As an example, let's imagine Jenny wishes to visit google.com.

1. Jenny first enters the URL of the website (google.com) in the browser on her local computer (the client).

2. Jenny's computer generates a *request* that is sent out to the server computer, which then accepts the *request*.

3. The server runs (or executes) the *back-end* code, usually grabbing data from (or querying) the database.

4. The database sends the requested data back to the server.

5. The server takes the data and executes the *front-end* code to produce a *response*.

6. This *response* is sent back out to the client where it is then displayed (or rendered) on the client computer as a standard web page.

Creation Phases of Web

Now that we've explored the fundamental process of how a web page is displayed to a user, we can dive into the deep end and discover where web development comes in and how it is applied to allow that magical ping pong-process to occur. As a broad definition, a web developer's primary purpose is to *create a functional website that performs a set of particular, defined functions.* Accomplishing this goal breaks down into three core phases.

Phase 1: Planning

During this preliminary phase, a web developer will work closely with the client and other developers to plan the structure and core concepts of the site. This first phase is an ideal time to decide how the various pages and components of the site link to one another (also known as a *sitemap*). While the *sitemap* can take on many forms, it should effectively outline how a *user* will navigate around the site. During the planning phase, it is also vital to determine how the *client* will interact with the site as well. If the client will be posting blogs or adding products to the online store component, it is the planning stage that should specify exactly how these tasks will be performed.

Phase 2: Design

The design phase is when the visual look and feel of the site is determined. This entails everything from color palette and fonts to page width and static image placement. If the planning phase determines *what* the user will do with the site, the design phase determines the *where* and the *how*. Typically a *mockup* for each page or component of the site is created in Photoshop by a designer or multi-disciplined developer. This *mockup* should typically include every visual element that is expected in the final page and is thus representative of what the client wants to see when visiting the website. Throughout the design process, it is critical to consider the target audience and demographic of the website. The design should closely correspond to both the appropriate user base the site is marketed toward as well as the intended use of the site.

For example, Google is intended for all audiences and emphasizes speed and efficiency of search results, which fits the minimalist design Google uses, including a visual look comprised of almost exclusively text. Netflix, on the other hand, is all about audio and visual content and thus focused on a very colorful, full-screen design to highlight the multitude of shows available on the platform.

Phase 3: Development

The development phase is of course the most crucial for web developers involved in the project, and where the majority of time and energy will be spent producing the final product. For most modern websites, the development process is broken down into three architectural components that the web developer will intermix throughout the procedure.

- Application Logic: Often referred to as the *model* component, this represents the majority of the back-end code a developer will write to make the site function as expected. This logic is also where a developer must understand and utilize the connection between the site and the database that powers it.

- Presentation: Commonly known as the *view* component, this is where the *mockup* that was created during the design phase is used by a developer to recreate the look and feel of the *mockup* image utilizing the basic building blocks of HTML and CSS, such that the end result is a webpage that looks identical to the *mockup*.

- Connection: Also referred to as the *controller* component, this code defines the connections between the back-end business logic that handles the grunt work of the site and the front-end pages that users will access: It connects the back- and front-end code together.

Website

Website is a collection of related web pages that may contain text, images, audio and video. The first page of a website is called home page. Each website has specific internet address (URL) that you need to enter in your browser to access a website.

Website is hosted on one or more servers and can be accessed by visiting its homepage using a computer network. A website is managed by its owner that can be an individual, company or an organization.

A website can be of two types:

- Static Website
- Dynamic Website

Static Website

Static website is the basic type of website that is easy to create. You don't need the knowledge of web programming and database design to create a static website. Its web pages are coded in HTML.

The codes are fixed for each page so the information contained in the page does not change and it looks like a printed page.

Static Website

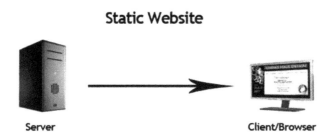

Server   Client/Browser

Dynamic Website

Dynamic website is a collection of dynamic web pages whose content changes dynamically. It accesses content from a database or Content Management System (CMS). Therefore, when you alter or update the content of the database, the content of the website is also altered or updated.

Dynamic website uses client-side scripting or server-side scripting, or both to generate dynamic content.

Client side scripting generates content at the client computer on the basis of user input. The web browser downloads the web page from the server and processes the code within the page to render information to the user.

In server side scripting, the software runs on the server and processing is completed in the server then plain pages are sent to the user.

Dynamic Website

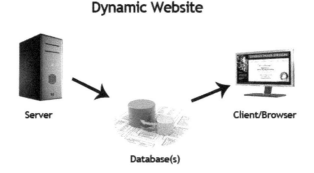

Server   Client/Browser

Database(s)

Static vs Dynamic website

Static Website	Dynamic Website
Prebuilt content is same every time the page is loaded.	Content is generated quickly and changes regularly.

It uses the HTML code for developing a website.	It uses the server side languages such as PHP,SERVLET, JSP, and ASP.NET etc. for developing a website.
It sends exactly the same response for every request.	It may generate different HTML for each of the request.
The content is only changed when someone publishes and updates the file (sends it to the web server).	The page contains "server-side" code which allows the server to generate the unique content when the page is loaded.
Flexibility is the main advantage of static website.	Content Management System (CMS) is the main advantage of dynamic website.

Various Types of Websites

Originally, websites were purely informational. Before the web was opened to the public, educational and research institutions and goverment agencies were able to make information available to each other via text-only websites. Now that we have the World Wide Web, there are more types of websites than you can shake a stick at.

1. Personal Websites

Your Internet Service Provider may offer you free server space for you to create your own website that might include some family photos and an online diary. Usually these will have a web address (URL) looking something like this: www.your-isp.com/~your-user-name/. This type of site is useful for a family, teenagers, grandparents, etc. to stay in touch with each other. This type is not advisable for a small business because the URL is not search engine friendly and the limited server capabilities your ISP offer may not be sophisticated enough for a small business website.

2. Photo Sharing Websites

These types of website are cropping up like fleas on dog. There are web companies like, Flickr.com, Photosite.com, and Google's Picasa. There could easily be over a hundred such sites that offer free photo sharing paid for by their online advertising. Also, many digital cameras and photo printers now come with software enabling mere mortals to create digital photo slide shows and upload them to the web.

3. Community Building Websites

These websites build online communities of people who want to interact with other people socially or meet people who share their interests. The best known website of this type is probably FaceBook.com. There is also Linkedin.com, and let's not forget the old MySpace.com just to mention a few. For sharing and discussing mutual interests, there are online forums for practically any subject you can think of. Forum websites can be a great source of information and help for the small business person. Now you can see this is where we start to get into the idea of "hybrid" sites. Photo Sharing sites might also be considered community building sites, much as Blogging sites are. Can Dating Sites be considered Community Building Sites, or are they E-commerce Sites. All that is up for discussion.

4. Mobile Device Websites

Although in its infancy, the use of mobile devices (cellphones, PDAs, iPods, iPhones, etc.) will become much more widespread and prevalent. One problem is that standard websites are difficult to view and take a long time to download on some of these devices with their small screens and wireless connections. Websites whose pages are narrower in width and take up less bandwidth work much better for mobile devices. A new domain designation has been created to identify websites that are "mobile friendly". That is .mobi, as in www.xislegraphix.mobi. If you have a small business that would benefit from being viewed on a mobile devise, you should consider investigating the possibilities now and get in on the ground floor of this trend that is only going to expand.

5. Blogging Websites

People took the words *Web Logs* and shortened it to *Blogs*—online diaries, journals, or editorials, if you will. My, how Blogs have taken over the internet. A person used to be outdated if he/she did not have a website, now having a blog is *de rigeur*. A blog owner will log-on daily, weekly, or whenever, and write about whatever is going on in their lives or business, or they may comment on politics and news. How wonderful the Internet is. Now anyone who can afford a blog can be self published and allow their thoughts to be read by anyone in the world who has online access.

6. Writers / Authors Websites

Writer's and Author's websites are part of what's known as the Writer's or Author's Platform in the publishing business. The platform includes, a website, a Facebook presence, blog, Twitter account, and the old fashioned mailing list. Many publishers will ask a prospective client about their platform. In other words, "If we publish your book, what sort of a reader base do you already have that we can count on to buy your new publication?" Fairly weighty request, wouldn't you say? For now, let's concentrate on the website part. A writers website would include a biography, a catalog of published books and works, perhaps excerpts from some works, links to publications on sites like Amazon.com, a link to the writer's blog, reviews and comments on the author's publications. You get the idea, and that is to build a following, a fan base to which future publications can be directly marketed.

7. Informational Websites

A major informational site is wikipedia.org, the online encyclopedia. And it is unique, because it allows visitors to contribute and edit articles. Now your small business may not want such a comprehensive site, but if you have information to share of sell, an informational website would fill the bill. Suppose you have a landscaping business. You could create a website that lists plants with their definitions and planting and caring instructions. This would be helpful to people, and you would use it to lead people to your nursery. Of course you could "hybrid" this site with e-commerce and also sell your plants online.

8. Online Business Brochure/Catalog Websites

In the days before the Internet, we used the print, radio, and television media to spread the word about our businesses. Now we can cast a large net, reaching literally millions of people with just one website. With your online brochure or catalog, you can show anyone who looks for and finds your website, photos and descriptions of your products or services. To some this may sound like an Ecommerce Website, but there are many businesses that deal in products or services that are not sellable over the web—think hair-stylist, dentist, or day-care center.

9. E-commerce Websites

Ever hear of Amazon.com? It's one of the grand-daddies of all ecommerce websites. But you don't have to be an Amazon to sell your products online. There are millions of small businesses who use their ecommerce websites to sell their products over the internet. Just about anything that can be sold in a brick-and-mortar store can be sold online—with much less overhead.

Web Server

A web server is a computer that runs websites. It's a computer program that distributes web pages as they are requisitioned. The basic objective of the web server is to store, process and deliver web pages to the users. This intercommunication is done using Hypertext Transfer Protocol (HTTP). These web pages are mostly static content that includes HTML documents, images, style sheets, test etc. Apart from HTTP, a web server also supports SMTP (Simple Mail transfer Protocol) and FTP (File Transfer Protocol) protocol for emailing and for file transfer and storage.

The main job of a web server is to display the website content. If a web server is not exposed to the public and is used internally, then it is called Intranet Server. When anyone requests for a website by adding the URL or web address on a web browser's (like Chrome or Firefox) address bar (like www.economictimes.com), the browser sends a request to the Internet for viewing the corresponding web page for that address. A Domain Name Server (DNS) converts this URL to an IP Address (For example 192.168.216.345), which in turn points to a Web Server.

The web server is requested to present the content website to the user's browser. All websites on the Internet have a unique identifier in terms of an IP address. This Internet Protocol address is used to communicate between different servers across the Internet. These days, Apache server is the most common web server available in the market. Apache is an open source software that handles almost 70 percent of all websites available today. Most of the web-based applications use Apache as their default Web Server environment. Another web server that is generally available is Internet Information Service (IIS). IIS is owned by Microsoft.

Web Server Working

Web server respond to the client request in either of the following two ways:

- Sending the file to the client associated with the requested URL.

- Generating response by invoking a script and communicating with database

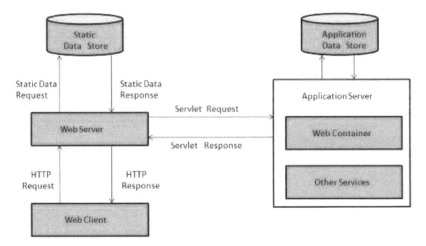

Key Points

- When client sends request for a web page, the web server search for the requested page if requested page is found then it will send it to client with an HTTP response.

- If the requested web page is not found, web server will the send an HTTP response:Error 404 Not found.

- If client has requested for some other resources then the web server will contact to the application server and data store to construct the HTTP response.

Architecture

Web server architecture follows the following two approaches:

1. Concurrent Approach
2. Single-Process-Event-Driven Approach.

Concurrent Approach

Concurrent approach allows the web server to handle multiple client requests at the same time. It can be achieved by following methods:

- Multi-process
- Multi-threaded
- Hybrid method.

Multi-processing

In this a single process (parent process) initiates several single-threaded child processes and distribute incoming requests to these child processes. Each of the child processes are responsible for handling single request.

It is the responsibility of parent process to monitor the load and decide if processes should be killed or forked.

Multi-threaded

Unlike Multi-process, it creates multiple single-threaded process.

Hybrid

It is combination of above two approaches. In this approach multiple process are created and each process initiates multiple threads. Each of the threads handles one connection. Using multiple threads in single process results in less load on system resources.

Examples

Following table describes the most leading web servers available today:

S.N.	Web Server Descriptino
1	**Apache HTTP Server** This is the most popular web server in the world developed by the Apache Software Foundation. Apache web server is an open source software and can be installed on almost all operating systems including Linux, UNIX, Windows, FreeBSD, Mac OS X and more. About 60% of the web server machines run the Apache Web Server.

2.	**Internet Information Services (IIS)**
	The Internet Information Server (IIS) is a high performance Web Server from Microsoft. This web server runs on Windows NT/2000 and 2003 platforms (and may be on upcoming new Windows version also). IIS comes bundled with Windows NT/2000 and 2003; Because IIS is tightly integrated with the operating system so it is relatively easy to administer it.
3.	**Lighttpd**
	The lighttpd, pronounced lighty is also a free web server that is distributed with the FreeBSD operating system. This open source web server is fast, secure and consumes much less CPU power. Lighttpd can also run on Windows, Mac OS X, Linux and Solaris operating systems.
4.	**Sun Java System Web Server**
	This web server from Sun Microsystems is suited for medium and large web sites. Though the server is free it is not open source. It however, runs on Windows, Linux and UNIX platforms. The Sun Java System web server supports various languages, scripts and technologies required for Web 2.0 such as JSP, Java Servlets, PHP, Perl, Python, and Ruby on Rails, ASP and Coldfusion etc.
5.	**Jigsaw Server**
	Jigsaw (W3C's Server) comes from the World Wide Web Consortium. It is open source and free and can run on various platforms like Linux, UNIX, Windows, and Mac OS X Free BSD etc. Jigsaw has been written in Java and can run CGI scripts and PHP programs.

Web Server Overload

The web server overload is quite a common issue regardless of an organization's experience in handling the server side matters. Even the popular sites like Facebook and YouTube have faced server crashes. Therefore, there is no wonder that you are struggling to deal with it, especially if you are new to this. Years of research and a number of case studies of the real-time scenario have come up with lots of points that include the causes of web server overload, signs, and finally, the preventive measures to control the future prospects.

Causes of Web Server Overload

At any time web servers can be overloaded due to the following reasons, such as mentioned under:

1. Web server's incomplete availability: This can happen because of expected or necessary support or update, hardware or software crashes, back-end malfunctions, etc. In these circumstances, rest of the web servers get too much traffic and grow overloaded.

2. Surplus local web traffic: Numerous clients which are connecting to the website within a brief interval may cause a web server overload. For instance, have you ever noticed that your university website hadn't loaded at all when your semester result had arrived? This causes sudden hike which is not for longer duration, either.

3. Computer worms and XSS viruses: These will cause irregular traffic due to millions of infected computers, browsers or web servers. Once these are released the network will significantly reduce its traffic.

4. Denial of Service/Distributed Denial of Service (DoS/DDoS) attacks – A denial-of-service attack or distributed denial-of-service attack is an effort to make a computer or network device unavailable to its proposed users. If one system is found vulnerable, it is targeted by multiple other systems. These other systems are too controlled by the hacker(s) who somehow breach(es) into the system security by guessing the right password. Overall, the network gets flooded by packets, that ultimately crashes the server leading it to deny the real requests.

5. Network slowdowns – So that client requests are completed more slowly and the number of connections increases so much that server limits are approached.

Signs of Web Server Overload

1. If overload results in a delayed serving of requests from 1 second to a few hundred seconds.

2. If the web server returns an HTTP error code, such as 500, 502, 503, 504, 408, etc. which are inappropriate overload conditions.

3. The web server denies or resets TCP connections before it returns any content.

4. Sometimes the server delivers only a part of the requested content. This can be studied as a bug, even if it normally occurs as a symptom of overload.

Ways to Prevent Web Server Overload

To partly master above average load limits and to prevent overload, several big websites practice standard techniques, as mentioned below:

1. By controlling network traffic, using Firewalls to block undesired traffic coming from poor IP sources, or having inadequate patterns. HTTP traffic managers can be placed to drop, redirect, or rewrite requests which have poor HTTP patterns. To smooth the peaks in the network usage bandwidth management and traffic shaping can be done.

2. By expanding web cache methods. The cache saves a lot of time. Instead of literally asking for the content from the literal server, that basically may reside far away from the client's native place, if a number of cache contents are made available, it would reduce the time to a great extent.

3. By implementing different domain names to subserve different contents by separating the web servers.

4. Employing different domain names or computers to separate big files from small and medium-sized files. The idea is to be able to fully cache small and medium-sized files and sufficiently serve big or huge files by using different settings.

5. By using many internet servers or programs per computer, each one should be connected to its own network card and IP address.

6. By using many computers that are arranged together behind a load balancer, so that they perform or are seen as one large web server.

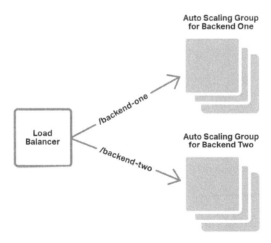

7. By combining more hardware devices to each computer. This improves the memory part, both primary and secondary. And also by tuning the OS parameters for hardware capacities and usage.

8. By adapting more efficient computer programs for web servers. It is mandatory to revise the existing technology that you use for your organization, so as to make it run smoothly with fewer difficulties.

9. By practicing other workarounds, particularly if dynamic content is included. The dynamic contents take more time as compared to static page contents because they change based on the user's requirements, geographic location, and get displayed accordingly.

The above practices may be held true for one condition and might not work for another case. This implies that the preventive methods are not hard core measures to combat. The trial and error method is the key to actually know what suits your server's needs.

Web Engineering

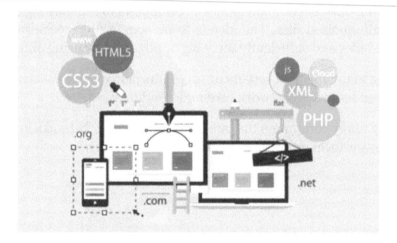

Web engineering is the application of systematic, disciplined and quantifiable approaches to development, operation, and maintenance of Web-based applications. It is both a pro-active approach and a growing collection of theoretical and empirical research in Web application development. This part gives an overview of web engineering by addressing the questions: a) why is it needed? b) what is its domain of operation? c) how does it help and what should it do to improve Web application development? and d) how should it be incorporated in education and training? The paper discusses the significant differences that exist between Web applications and conventional software, the taxonomy of Web applications, the progress made so far and the research issues and experience of creating a specialisation at the master's level. The it reaches a conclusion that Web Engineering at this stage is a moving target since Web technologies are constantly evolving, making new types of applications possible, which in turn may require innovations in how they are built, deployed and maintained.

Web Engineering is the application of systematic, disciplined and quantifiable approaches to development, operation, and maintenance of Web-based applications. It is a response to the early, chaotic development of Web sites and applications as well as recognition of a divide between web developers and conventional software developers. Viewed broadly, web engineering is both a conscious and pro-active approach and a growing collection of theoretical and empirical research. Special issues of journals, an edited book of papers , series of workshops, tutorials and special tracks at international conferences, and dedicated international conferences attest to the level of activity in this field. However, this list is only a partial representation of the work undertaken in the field and the experiences of the multitude of Web developers. The practice, good and bad, is leading the theory, to quote a remark made about the field of software maintenance a few years ago.

The need for Web Engineering is felt (or dismissed) according to perceptions of the developers and managers, their experiences in creating applications made feasible by the new technologies, and the complexity of Web applications. In the early stages of Web development, White and Powell, identified and emphasized the need for engineering as in Web Document Engineering and Web Site Engineering. Web Engineering, more generally, explicitly recognises the fact that good Web development requires multidisciplinary efforts and does not fit neatly into any of the existing disciplines.

Perceptions of Web Development

Web development is perceived at different levels, shown in figure.

6. Web project planning and management
5. Web-based System
4. Web Site Construction
3. Web Site Design
2. Web Page Design
1. Web Page Construction

Figure: Levels of perception in Web Development

For someone relatively new to Web development, be they developers, users or managers, the Web is manifested through the Web pages, the outcome of the simplest and most visible level. It also happens to be the easiest to understand and master since it is built upon a mark-up language (HTML) rather than a programming language. The next level, Web Page Design, becomes apparent as the developers and managers gain experience. If they are from information technology (IT) background they realise that special skills are required, many outside computer science itself, the background of software engineers. The non-IT managers and developers, on the other hand, may not start to appreciate the crucial role of programming, databases, networks and other IT areas till later. The page design, though, may not be regarded as problematic since there are many packages that promise to ease the burden of page design. In software engineering terms, these two levels correspond to user interface, generally regarded as a matter of detail and lying more in human computer interaction (HCI) arena. The next level of perception regards Web Site Design or Information Architecture for some. Here, the hypertextual nature of the Web comes into play, since good web sites provide good navigation structures (i.e., structures that help its users achieve their goals). This level has not been addressed at all by traditional software engineering, and again may involve skills outside computer science. In figure above, only levels 4 to 6 deal with processes of interest to software engineers.

To add to the perceptual difficulties here, a large number of organisations enter the Web development at stage 3, i.e. by decreeing that they must have a Web presence. Consequently, Web development may be viewed mainly in terms of publishing or brand building/reinforcement, where lessons learnt from software engineering are regarded as irrelevant or simply ignored. The understanding and importance of other stages become clearer only after a Web site is created, and the realization that it is, after all, an information system. The need for systematic, measurable and repeatable development processes then becomes apparent. Late recognition of the importance of Web Engineering could then lead to a redesign and re-engineering of the existing sites and applications, resulting in wasted efforts and resources.

Thus, software engineering is applicable and necessary at the application and project management levels but is not sufficient for all the activities as depicted in figure above. Further, there is a consensus, explained below, that even where software engineering is applicable, more and newer development, testing and maintenance methods will have to be found to deal with specific problems of Web development.

Web Developers' Experience, New Technologies and Expert Consensus

The need for Web Engineering has been debated and discussed in several fora, including each workshop and conference mentioned above. Published contributions come from many sources, conference and workshop proceedings, journal articles, special issues of IEEE Multimedia, Cutter IT Journal, IEEE Software and IEEE Internet Computing, and the edited book on Web Engineering. From these discussions, It is fair to say that the importance of and need for Web Engineering is now reasonably established, through a consensus among experts on the major differences in the characteristics of Web applications and conventional. As the authors note, these differences do not arise simply due to the fact that many, early Web developers came from non-software engineering background but because of the new types of (Web) applications. They have all commented on the similarities in application development problems when software engineering was first proposed and the present time in relation to Web development.

Table: Major Differences between Web Applications and Conventional Software

Web applications	Conventional software
1. compressed development schedules	2. constant evolution with shortened revision cycles
3. "content is king", i.e. it is integrated inextricably with procedural processing	4. insufficient requirement specifications
5. small teams working to very short schedules	6. emerging technologies/methodologies
7. lack of accepted testing processes	8. user satisfaction and the threat from one's competition
9. minimal management support	10. criticality of performance
11. evolving standards to which Web applications should or must comply, depending on the specific circumstances (for example accessibility standards for government sites or IEEE or W3C standards for technological reasons).	12. understanding of additional disciplines required for Web applications, such as hypertext, graphic design, information architecture
13. security considerations	14. legal, social and ethical issues
15. variety of backgrounds of developers	16. Rapidly evolving implementation environment, encompassing various hardware platforms

Table above summarises the experts' findings with a few additional, distinctive characteristics. It is worth noting that this enumeration is based on the experiences of Web developers that the experts had consulted. Once the differences were identified, the question was raised as to whether current software engineering practices could address them successfully. The consensus was that software engineering was needed but was not enough by itself.

Two points are worth elaborating. They both arise from the raison díetre of the Web, viz. communicating information on a global scale. Table includes them. The first is the nature of information ("content is king") and its effect on the development of a Web application. The second one is the nature of end-users ("user satisfaction and threat of competition") of Web applications.

With regard to information, information systems until now have dealt with largely transactional data in predominantly numerical form, with a bit of textual information, which can be more easily normalised, structured, sorted and searched. Web-based information systems contain text and multimedia, which are difficult to structure, cannot be normalised and are very hard to sort and search. Furthermore, they mix document-orientation with database access through the hypertext metaphor. As content, they are at this time 'integrated inextricably with procedural processing' (part of 'content is king', above). Furthermore, they raise questions of information ownership, and are mired in matters of legal, ethical, social and legal issues. Software developers did not deal with these issues in the past. Web developers must take them into account in creating Web applications. The implication is that if proper policies and procedures are not created, the work of Web developers may not achieve what the client wants.

Regarding the nature of the end-users, Web applications may address users anywhere in the world. Unlike the systems in use until now, the Web-based ones are not always confined to specific user groups within an organisation. If Web applications were limited to intranets, the difficulties in understanding the users would be minimised. If they go beyond intranets, however, strategies and policies must be developed to better understand the potential, unknown, and perhaps unknowable, users to establish the quality parameters of the applications in order to deliver quality systems, test sites and applications and maintain security.

Characteristics and Complexity of Web Applications

Web applications vary widely: from small-scale, short-lived services to large-scale enterprise applications distributed across the Internet and corporate intranets. Over the years, Web applications have evolved and become more complex ñ they range from simple, read-only applications, to full-fledged information systems. This complexity may be in terms of performance (number of hits per second), for example the Slashdot site, the Olympics sites receiving hundreds of thousands of hits per minute, or in terms of dynamic nature of information, the use of multimedia or in other ways. They may provide vast, dynamic information in multiple media formats (graphics, images and video) or may be relatively simple. Nevertheless, they all demand balance between information content, aesthetics and performance. Table, below, brings out the characteristics of early, simple Web-based systems and current, advanced Web-based systems.

Multidisciplinary Nature of Web Development

Web applications handle information in its myriad forms (text, graphics, video, audio). Information sciences, multimedia, hypermedia and graphic design deal with structuring, processing, storing and presenting this information. Human-computer Interaction (HCI) and requirements engineering are essential to understand users and their requirements. Network management, general computing and simulation and modelling are required to deliver the information and desired functionality with an acceptable performance level. Software engineering, including new development methodologies, is essential for project and process management. Since information is very often published for worldwide access, publishing paradigm, and legal, social and ethical issues have to be taken on board. Consequently, good Web development must utilise relevant parts of all these disciplines and not be dominated by narrow viewpoints. Web Engineering is a response in recognition of this multidisciplinary nature of Web applications. Interestingly, the ACM Computing Curricula formulates its first principle with a similar statement by stating that "Computing extends well beyond the boundaries of computer science". However, their recommendations cover the entire computing area whereas Web Engineering concentrates on Web development.

| Table: Characteristics of Simple and Advanced Web Applications ||
Simple Web-based systems	Advanced Web-based systems
• Primarily textual information in non-core applications • Information content fairly static • Simple navigation • Infrequent access or limited usefulness • Limited interactivity and functionality. Stand alone systems • High performance not a major requirement • Developed by a single individual or by a very small team • Security requirements minimal (because of mainly one-way flow of information) • Easy to create • Feedback from users either unnecessary or not sought • Web site mainly as an ëidentityí for the current clientele, and not as a medium for communication	• Dynamic Web pages because information changes with time and users needs • Large volume of information • Difficult to navigate and find information • Integrated with database and other planning, scheduling and tracking systems • Deployed in mission-critical applications • Prepared for seamless evolution • High performance and continuous availability is a necessity • May require a larger development team with expertise in diverse areas • Calls for risk or security assessment and management • Needs configuration control and management • Necessitates project plan and management • Requires a sound development process and methodology • User satisfaction vital • Web site/application as the main communication medium between the organization and users

Evolution and Taxonomy of Web Applications

| Table: Categories of Web Applications ||
Category	Examples
• Informational	Online newspapers, product catalogues, newsletters, service manuals, classifieds, e-books

• Interactive
   ▪ # User-provided information
   ▪ # Customized acces
	Registration forms, customized information presentation, games

• Transaction	E-shopping, ordering goods and services, banking
• ! Workflow	Planning and scheduling systems, inventory management, status monitoring
• Collaborative work environments	Distributed authoring systems, collaborative design tools
• Online communities, marketplaces	Chat groups, recommender systems, marketplaces, auctions
• Web Portals	Electronic shopping malls, intermediaries
• Web Services	Enterprise applications, information and business intermediaries

The take-up of Web technologies and applications within an organisation will not necessarily follow the way the Web has evolved. Specifically, the World Wide Web was created to solve a specific problem of disseminating information. However, it opened up a novel way of communication and the developers stretched the technologies to make the applications interactive, forcing, in turn, further, rapid innovations in technologies. It also spawned a new client-server architecture that has become the environment of choice for many applications, both in the Internet and in intranets. The result of this leap-frogging is a wide variety of Web applications, technologies, tools, techniques and methods. The Web is now used to deal with problems in many domains, traditional as well as completely new. An organisation may, therefore, start its own Web development anywhere in the spectrum outlined in table. The need for Web Engineering has been argued above but how successful it is in delivering Web applications to a satisfactory level will be contingent upon matching the problem domains properly to solution methods and the relevant mix of technologies. In that sense, web engineering is essentially about problem solving. Webís legacy as an information medium rather than an application medium leads some people to regard Web development primarily as an authoring and publishing problem, giving rise to statements such as Web development is an art or it is only media manipulation and presentation. The first category of Web applications, 'informational' may seem to fall in this domain, although even with them it will be erroneous to underestimate the total effort and the need to systematise the development work. In any case, this taxonomy should clarify to both organizations and developers that there is a far greater range of Web applications and help them to map out a strategy for Web development within an organisation. One of the tasks in Web Engineering is to match appropriate methods, technologies (and tools and techniques) to each of these domains.

Need for Web Engineering

The need for Web Engineering is felt (or dismissed) according to perceptions of the developers and managers, their experiences in creating applications made feasible by the new technologies, and the complexity of Web applications. In the early stages of Web development, White and Powell, identified and emphasized the need for engineering as in Web Document Engineering and Web Site Engineering.

Web development within an organisation depends upon several factors. The motivation depends upon the initial purpose of using the Web (Web 'presence' or becoming a Web-based organisation), the customers expectations and the competitive environment The drive to systematise development is subject to overall perception of the Web, as depicted in figure above, and conscious policy decisions within the organisation. For example, a low level perception of the Web is likely to lead to ad hoc, sporadic efforts. As a starting point in understanding the problem domains that the Web currently can address, Table above presents taxonomy of Web applications updated after Ginige and Murugesan. The order of these categories roughly illustrates the evolution of Web applications. Organisations that started their Web development early may also have followed a similar order in the past. Although, it is possible to start Web development with applications in any category, this table has been useful to explain to organisations with modest presence on the Web how they might improve or benefit from incremental exposure, thus keeping the risks to the minimum12. development requires multidisciplinary efforts and does not fit neatly into any of the existing disciplines.

Practice and Research Issues in Developing, Testing and Maintaining Web Applications (Web Engineering)

While there are many differences between Web development and Software development, there are also similarities between them. These include:

- need for methodologies,
- requirements elicitation,
- programming,
- testing, and
- maintenance of those parts that deal with programming and functionalities.

Web Engineering has much to learn from software engineering in these areas but, in the light of the differences enumerated before, software engineering methods may have to be modified or new methods devised.

However, there is one major difference that Web developers/engineers have to bear in mind, as the discussion below clarifies. Web development, and in particular, Web site creation and maintenance, are not merely technical activities. Software development is generally regarded as the province of computing professionals. Web development affects the entire organization, including its interfaces with the world, and has to accommodate non-developers, especially management, when designing or recommending architecture and policies. This is particularly true of content management

Methodologies

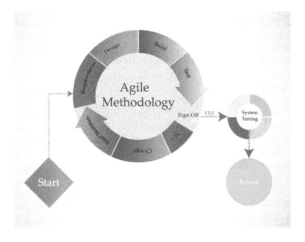

A recent survey on Web-based project highlights serious problems plaguing large Web-based projects:

- Delivered systems did not meet business needs 84% of the time.

- Schedule delays plagued the projects 79% of the time.

- Projects exceeded the budget 63% of the time

- Delivered system didnít have required functionality 53% of the time.

- Deliverables were of poor quality 52 % of time.

Another survey explicitly reported on the usage of multimedia and Web development techniques and methodologies to suggest that: a) no uniform approach existed, and b) developers need new techniques to do their job.

A caveat is in order. Given the nature of Statistics, the surveys may be statistically valid only for the population they were based on. This is not to question the findings here and a statistical critique of the surveys is beyond the scope of this paper.

At the same time, it is only fair to acknowledge that anecdotal evidence, gathered through personal experience and informal discussions through all the fora cited at the beginning of this paper do point to a wider horizon where the results of both the surveys are borne out. There is also support for this conclusion in the form of absence of a large collection of successful case studies where a systematic approach to Web development was followed and replicated.

Web Engineering has to and aims to improve on this. To this end, several methodologies have been proposed and the experience of their use reported as case studies. For example, for OOHDM, Ceri et al on WebML, Lowe and Henderson-Sellers on OPEN Space Framework, Goeschka and Schranz on their object-oriented engineering framework, Kirda on their adaptation of RMM31 and Conallen on extending the UML. The description and critique of these and other methodologies are beyond the scope of this paper. Section 2 mentioned small teams working to very short schedules as characteristics of Web applications. This is inevitably going to lead to evolutionary approaches to developing such applications. Agile methods and eXtreme programming address similar problems. .

The attraction of the Web and easy availability of development tools have also led to a mushrooming of sites and applications created by end-users, rather than by professionals. The growth in end-user computing logically leads to concerns about the quality and reliability of such applications. Interestingly, but not surprisingly, the Web-based developments have aroused similar concerns from practitioners in other disciplines, who see the Web site and application developers disregarding their traditions and proven techniques The methodological papers cited before report success of a planned, systematic approach in specific case studies but their repeatability is not fully established nor are their approaches compared with other methods. It is therefore difficult to estimate if the reported successes should be attributed to the generic nature of the proposed methods or to the expertise of the authors who have found methods that work for them.

Engineering is about systematic, disciplined and quantifiable approaches to create usable systems. Among the hallmarks of these approaches are measurability and repeatability of work. Software engineers and other IT professionals lament the fact that software industry is not strong on either. Measurements are scarce and repeatability is exercised more by experience and intuition. There is tremendous opportunity for Web Engineering community to get things right in this arena.

Apart from devising methodologies, a legitimate field of research, Web developers and researchers need to report empirical results of what worked under which circumstances and if it did not, why

Requirements Elicitation

Insufficient requirements specifications and constant evolution were cited as two major differences between Web applications and other software. User-centric approaches and methods to build applications have an unrealised potential in arriving at better specifications. The openness of the Web makes it feasible to get user feedback (and requirements) on-line as opposed to more laborious and expensive traditional methods, such as meetings, interviews, paper-based surveys and focus groups. The on-line methods have not been tried out yet in any great measure and could prove to be very interesting. It is also likely that users now will have a greater say in application development.

Testing, Metrics and Quality

Web testing has many dimensions11, 36 in addition to conventional software testing. Each unit of a Web application such as page, code, site, navigation, standards, legal requirements must be tested. Usability testing has also become a big and somewhat controversial issue37. Services like W3C's HTML, CSS and XHTML certification, and Bobby for accessibility are freely available to Web developers. Consultants in Web site auditing also provide a testing service. However, Web engineers need to create explicit testing strategies that include the relevant tests.

Web metrics and quality are interlinked38, 39, and like software metrics, under-utilised. However, more tools are becoming available and Web engineers need to evolve conscious policies to test their sites and applications.

Maintenance

Web maintenance, even more than software maintenance, is a continuous activity. Depending on the nature of the application, the maintenance can become quite complex and does not solely reside in the technical domain. Apart from the evolutionary aspect of Web applications, dealt with in the previous sub-sections, the major differences between Web application and software maintenance arise in relation to content management and site navigation. Content generation, and hence its update and maintenance, will necessarily vary across organisations and applications. The allocation of responsibilities for content may be carried out by human resources (as job descriptions) or other, general management units40. Nevertheless, it is imperative that Web developers detail how content maintenance should be carried out and, more importantly, influence the relevant policies.

Web Design

Web design is the process of creating websites. It encompasses several different aspects, including webpage layout, content production, and graphic design. While the terms web design and web development are often used interchangeably, web design is technically a subset of the broader category of web development.

Websites are created using a markup language called HTML. Web designers build webpages using HTML tags that define the content and metadata of each page. The layout and appearance of the elements within a webpage are typically defined using CSS, or cascading style sheets. Therefore, most websites include a combination of HTML and CSS that defines how each page will appear in a browser.

Some web designers prefer to hand code pages (typing HTML and CSS from scratch), while others use a "WYSIWYG" editor like Adobe Dreamweaver. This type of editor provides a visual interface for designing the webpage layout and the software automatically generates the corresponding HTML and CSS code. Another popular way to design websites is with a content management system like WordPress or Joomla. These services provide different website templates that can be used as a starting point for a new website. Webmasters can then add content and customize the layout using a web-based interface.

While HTML and CSS are used to design the look and feel of a website, images must be created separately. Therefore, graphic design may overlap with web design, since graphic designers often create images for use on the Web. Some graphics programs like Adobe Photoshop even include a "Save for Web" option that provides an easy way to export images in a format optimized for web publishing.

Elements of Web Design

Web design uses many of the same key visual elements as all types of design such as:

Layout: This is the way the graphics, ads and text are arranged. In the web world, a key goal is to help the view find the information they seek at a glance. This includes maintaining the balance, consistency, and integrity of the design.

Colour: The choice of colours depends on the purpose and clientele; it could be simple black-and-white to multi-coloured design, conveying the personality of a person or the brand of an organization, using web-safe colours.

Graphics: Graphics can include logos, photos, clipart or icons, all of which enhance the web design. For user friendliness, these need to be placed appropriately, working with the colour and content of the web page, while not making it too congested or slow to load.

Fonts: The use of various fonts can enhance a website design. Most web browsers can only read a select number of fonts, known as "web-safe fonts", so your designer will generally work within this widely accepted group.

Content: Content and design can work together to enhance the message of the site through visuals and text. Written text should always be relevant and useful, so as not to confuse the reader and to give them what they want so they will remain on the site. Content should be optimized for search engines and be of a suitable length, incorporating relevant keywords.

Creating User-Friendly Web Design

Besides the basic elements of web design that make a site beautiful and visually compelling, a website must also always consider the end user. User-friendliness can be achieved by paying attention to the following factors.

Navigation: Site architecture, menus and other navigation tools in the web design must be created with consideration of how users browse and search. The goal is to help the user to move around the site with ease, efficiently finding the information they require.

Multimedia: Relevant video and audio stimuli in the design can help users to grasp the information, developing understanding in an easy and quick manner. This can encourage visitors to spend more time on the webpage.

Compatibility: Design the webpage, to perform equally well on different browsers and operating systems, to increase its viewing.

Technology: Advancements in technology give designers the freedom to add movement and innovation, allowing for web design that is always fresh, dynamic and professional.

Interactive: Increase active user participation and involvement, by adding comment boxes and opinion polls in the design. Convert users from visitors to clients with email forms and newsletter sign-ups.

Web Content Development

Web content development is the procedure of researching & gathering valuable information, defining objectives, finding & evaluating keywords to be used & organizing the structure for writing & finally publishing a content.

Undoubtedly, in the world of internet and web development, content is the king. Content is the medium through which you can provide interesting and valuable information to your audience. By providing well optimized information, your content becomes visible by search engines, increases ranking results and therefore it is easily found and read.

Steps for Effective Web Content Development

1. Researching & Analysing Competition

Specify your competitors & extract information from competitors' sources, regarding the subject you want to write about. Gather as much information as you can! The initial research will help you significantly find ideas concerning which keywords to use when developing your content.

2. Defining Objectives

You must specify the main goals (products or services) that need to be promoted through your content (blog post, article, image, video or other interactive forms). If the content to be developed refers to a website, then define the pages of your website that need to be optimized. It is really important and take it into serious consideration, that each page of the website needs to be optimized for unique keywords / keyword phases that are related to one and only subject.

3. Finding & Evaluating Keywords to be used

Make a list of possible keyword phrases that are going to be used for the optimized content. If you are going to create content for a website, then make a different list of keywords, for each page you are going to optimize. The keyword phases listed should be both head terms and long tailed ones. Be inspired from:

The initial research you have performed & the objectives & goals you have set. Ask yourself:

- Which are the keywords / keyword phrases that best describe the product or service that needs to be promoted?

- What kind of terms have you found through the competitors' sources that can be used to describe the relevant product or service?

- Which terms do your competitors use? Be careful to select only those keywords that are highly relative to your goals and objectives. And the fact that you are selecting them for your initial list does not necessarily mean that you are going to use them as well. The list will be finalized after evaluating keywords performance

- If you were a user, which search terms would you choose to use in order to find the specific promoted information?

Google analytics account excluding the branded terms. In the organic results, exclude the branded terms and narrow down your keywords list with the keywords that have brought the highest traffic.

PPC keywords (Pay Per Click) provided by Google Analytics. Write down the PPC keywords that have generated the most traffic.

So, after you have ended up with a list of keywords: Use an effective keyword tool such as google adwords Keyword Tool or the very effective Keyword Research tool of Web SEO Analytics and check your keyword phrases performance. The greater the number of searches is, the more popular a keyword is. The greater the competition is the more difficult it is to easily gain good ranking results for the specific keyword phrases.

After the research, select the best keywords / keyword phrases that define your content according to relevancy & query popularity.

Then, use the Keyword Difficulty of Web SEO Analytics so as to evaluate the possibilities of achieving good rankings for each of the selected keywords.

By combining both the Keyword Research and Keyword Difficulty tools you will be able not only to find all the popular keywords that are related to your specific subject but also to decide on the keywords with which you will more likely accomplish high rankings in search engine results.

After you have ended up with the final list of the top keywords, try to spread them through the content accordingly.

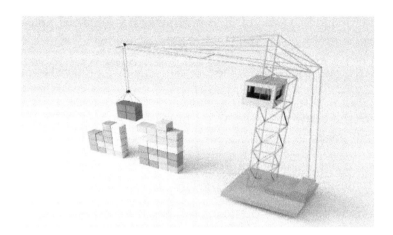

4. Organising the Structure

a. There is no ideal number of times to use a keyword on a web page. And if this still remains confusing, it is advisable that the density of each keyword/keyword phrase should not be more than 3 times, per 300 words (e.g. page of a website). The key is to make the selected keyword phrases appear naturally inside the content of each page and at a reasonable rate.

b. Try to use the specific keywords / keyword phrases on important positions inside the page such as:

- The URL

- The title

- The first sentence or at least the first paragraph

- Headings and subheadings

- Image file names and alt texts

- Meta (title, description, keywords)

- Text links to related content inside the website

Web Content Developer

A web content writer is responsible for creating original content for websites, newsletters, press releases, blogs, articles and advertising and marketing materials based on the requirements of a client/organization. Content developers often use their skills, knowledge and experience in software and programming as well as web-based technology, to create and update content for websites.

Content development could involve creative work, such as copy writing or graphics, or technical work. Quite often, qualifications required for career as a content writer may vary. Hence, it is essential to keep yourselves updated with the latest technology trends to ensure on-going success. Self-employed content developers will have to attract and maintain a good client base to be successful in the long-term. Content development is basically about developing good content in a clear and presentable form. Hence, a content developer needs to have excellent command over written English. He/she should create web content based on analytical reports, press releases or survey reports and present them in a lucid, simple, easy to understand language.

Web Accessibility

Web accessibility means that people with disabilities can perceive, understand, navigate, and interact with the Web, and that they can contribute to the Web. Web accessibility also benefits others, including older people with changing abilities due to aging.

People with Disabilities on the Web

Though estimates vary, most studies find that about one fifth (20%) of the population has some kind of disability. Not all of these people have disabilities that make it difficult for them to access the internet, but it is still a significant portion of the population. Businesses would be unwise to purposely exclude 20, 10, or even 5 percent of their potential customers from their web sites. For schools, universities, and government entities it would not only be unwise, but in many cases, it would also violate the law.

Each of the major categories of disabilities requires certain types of adaptations in the design of web content. Most of the time, these adaptations benefit nearly everyone, not just people with disabilities. Almost everyone benefits from helpful illustrations, properly-organized content, and clear navigation. Similarly, while captions are a necessity for deaf users, they can be helpful to others, including anyone who views a video without audio.

Implementing Web Accessibility

Before anyone can make their web site accessible, they must understand accessibility, be committed to ensuring accessibility, learn how to implement accessibility, and understand their legal obligations.

Commitment and Accountability

Awareness: The foundation of any kind of commitment to web accessibility is awareness of the issues. Most web developers are not opposed to the concept of making the internet accessible to people with disabilities. Most accessibility errors on web sites are the result of lack of awareness, rather than malice or apathy.

Leadership: Understanding the issues is an important first step, but it does not solve the problem, especially in large organizations. If the leadership of an organization does not express commitment to web accessibility, chances are low that the organization's web content will be accessible. Oftentimes, a handful of developers make their own content accessible while the majority don't bother to, since it is not expected of them.

Policies and Procedures: Even when leaders express their commitment to an idea, if the idea is not backed up by policy, the idea tends to get lost among the day-to-day routines. The best approach for a large organization is to create an internal policy that outlines specific standards, procedures, and methods for monitoring compliance.

Training and Technical Support

Sometimes web developers fear that it is more expensive and time-consuming to create accessible web sites than it is to create inaccessible ones. This fear is largely untrue. The benefits of providing access to a larger population almost always outweigh the time required by a knowledgeable developer to implement that accessibility.

A developer can learn the basics of web accessibility in just a few days, but, as with any technical skill, it often takes months to internalize the mind set as well as the techniques. Online resources, such as the WebAIM articles, resources, email discussion list, monthly newsletter, and blog provide relevant resources for administrators, developers, and designers. There are many professionals that can help your organization ensure high accessibility. WebAIM offers onsite training, consulting & technical assistance, accessible site design, and other services.

Principles of Accessible Design

Below you will find a list of some key principles of accessible design. Most accessibility principles can be implemented very easily and will not impact the overall "look and feel" of your web site.

Provide Appropriate Alternative Text

Alternative text provides a textual alternative to non-text content in web pages. It is especially helpful for people who are blind and rely on a screen reader to have the content of the website read to them.

Provide Appropriate Document Structure

Headings, lists, and other structural elements provide meaning and structure to web pages. They can also facilitate keyboard navigation within the page.

Provide Headers for Data Tables

Tables are used online for layout and to organize data. Tables that are used to organize tabular data should have appropriate table headers (the <th> element). Data cells should be associated with their appropriate headers, making it easier for screen reader users to navigate and understand the data table.

Ensure users Can Complete and Submit All Forms

Ensure that every form element (text field, checkbox, dropdown list, etc.) has a label and make sure that label is associated to the correct form element using the <label> element. Also make sure the user can submit the form and recover from any errors, such as the failure to fill in all required fields.

Ensure Links Make Sense Out of Context

Every link should make sense if the link text is read by itself. Screen reader users may choose to read only the links on a web page. Certain phrases like "click here" and "more" must be avoided.

Caption and/or Provide Transcripts for Media

Videos and live audio must have captions and a transcript. With archived audio, a transcription may be sufficient.

Ensure accessibility of non-HTML content, including PDF files, Microsoft Word documents, PowerPoint presentations and Adobe Flash content.

In addition to all of the other principles listed here, PDF documents and other non-HT-

ML content must be as accessible as possible. If you cannot make it accessible, consider using HTML instead or, at the very least, provide an accessible alternative. PDF documents should also include a series of tags to make it more accessible. A tagged PDF file looks the same, but it is almost always more accessible to a person using a screen reader.

Allow users to Skip Repetitive Elements on the Page

You should provide a method that allows users to skip navigation or other elements that repeat on every page. This is usually accomplished by providing a "Skip to Main Content," or "Skip Navigation" link at the top of the page which jumps to the main content of the page.

Do not Rely on Color Alone to Convey Meaning

The use of color can enhance comprehension, but do not use color alone to convey information. That information may not be available to a person who is colorblind and will be unavailable to screen reader users.

Make Sure Content is Clearly Written and Easy to Read

There are many ways to make your content easier to understand. Write clearly, use clear fonts, and use headings and lists appropriately.

Make JavaScript Accessible

Ensure that JavaScript event handlers are device independent (e.g., they do not require the use of a mouse) and make sure that your page does not rely on JavaScript to function.

Design to Standards

HTML compliant and accessible pages are more robust and provide better search engine optimization. Cascading Style Sheets (CSS) allow you to separate content from presentation. This provides more flexibility and accessibility of your content.

References

- Web-development: techterms.com, Retrieved 16 May 2018
- What-web-accessibility: nomensa.com, Retrieved 14 June 2018
- Who-is-a-content-developer-and-what-are-the-basic-skills-and-qualifications-required-for-the-job-5008: zyxware.com, Retrieved 20 July 2018
- What-is-web-development: codingdojo.com, Retrieved 24 July 2018
- Website-static-vs-dynamic: javatpoint.com, Retrieved 23 March 2018
- 4-steps-for-effective-web-content-development: webseoanalytics.com, Retrieved 08 May 2018

3

Web Design

The use of different skills and disciplines for the production and maintenance of a website is called web design. This chapter has been carefully written to provide an easy understanding of the varied facets of web design such as user experience design, user interface design, flash, motion graphics, etc.

Web design is the planning and creation of websites. This includes a number of separate skills that all fall under the umbrella of web design. Some examples of these skills are information architecture, user interface, site structure, navigation, layout, colors, fonts and overall imagery. All of these skills are combined with the principles of design to create a website that meets the goals of the company or individual from whom that site is being created.

Parts of Web Design

Design, obviously, is a key part of "web design." What does this mean exactly? Design includes both the principles of design balance, contrast, emphasis, rhythm and unity and the design elements — lines, shapes, texture, color, and direction.

By putting these things together, a web designer creates websites, but a good web designer understands not only the principals of design but also the constraints of the Web. For example, a successful web designer will be skilled in typographic design principals, while also understanding the challenges of web type design and specifically how it differs from other kinds of type design.

In addition to understanding the limitations of the Web, a successful web professional also has a firm grasp on the strengths of digital communication.

Roles of Web Design

When you work as a web designer, you may be tasked with creating (or working on) entire sites or just individual pages and there is a lot to learn to be a well-rounded designer, including the following:

- HTML: this is the structure of web pages, creating the foundation of all websites.

- CSS: this is how web pages are visually styled. CSS (Cascading Style Sheets) handles the entire look of sites, including layout, typography, colors, and more.

- JavaScript: this governs certain behaviors on websites and can be used for a variety of interactions and features.

- CGI programming: CGI, and the next few entries (PHP, ASP, etc.) are all different flavors of programming languages. Many sites do not require any of these languages, but sites that are more feature-rich will certainly need to be coded using some of these languages.

- PHP, ASP, ColdFusion scripting.

- XML.

- Information architecture - the way a site's content and navigation is structured and presented helps make for a successful site that is easy and intuitive to use.

- SEO: Search engine optimization ensures that websites are attractive to Google and other search engines and that people looking for the products, services, or information features on that site can find it once they look for it online.

- Server management - all websites need to be hosted. The management of the servers that host those sites is an important web design skill.

- Web strategy and marketing - having a website is not enough. Those sites will also need to be marketed with an ongoing digital strategy.

- E-commerce and conversions.

- Design: creating the visual look and feel of websites has always been an important aspect of the industry.

- Speed: a successful site is one that loads quickly on a wide variety of devices, regardless of a visitors connection speed. Being able to tune the performance of sites is a very valuable skill.

- Content: people come to websites for the content that those sites contain. Being able to create that content is a critically important component in the world of website design.

New Skills in Web Design

Modular Design

As screen sizes multiply, the contexts we design for are changing. What we need are 'content building blocks' that adapt themselves to any environment. Learning about modular, reusable fragments of content as a basis for design helps us create content that fits any situation, which is a powerful skill to have.

Typographic Principles

"95 per cent of the information on the web is written language, " says information architect Oliver Reichenstein. "It's only logical to say that a web designer should get good training in the main discipline of shaping written information. In other words, typography."

Reichenstein raises a good point. However, we would argue that understanding 'the craft of words' should take priority. Words are an essential design element and, as designers of content, we often find ourselves working with language. A little time spent learning about language and how it can shape user experiences can go a long way.

Prototyping Tools

Digital prototyping tools have come of age over the last few years, and the opportunities in this space are developing rapidly. Tools like InVision, Marvel and Principle (not to mention Adobe's soon-to-be-unveiled Project Comet) enable designers to create fully fledged digital prototypes, quickly and easily.

If your focus is on the frontend, the ability to design and prototype websites and mobile apps, from wireframe to finished product, is extremely valuable. I'd strongly recommend diving in and acquiring some new knowledge.

This progression in tooling also means that designers focused on designing complex, interactive products now have the tools at their disposal to turn their visions into rich prototypes – complete with an emphasis on user interaction and also, importantly, animation and transitions.

Of course, understanding the fundamentals of what is possible (and what is codable) is important.

Animation Principles

Animation is increasingly expected in the interfaces we design. "Subtle animations and interactions, used well, can be the difference between an app or site that's feeling native, seamless and engaging, and one that is static and unintuitive, " states designer Dan Edwards.

Understanding the principles that underpin animation – ideas like timing, easing and spatial awareness – is becoming increasingly important.

There are a number of helpful tools that allow you to work on animation within an interaction design context, and exploring these is going to become increasingly helpful for designers. Tools like After Effects, Framer and Atomic will become a valuable part of the designers' toolbox.

SVGs

Scalable Vector Graphics (SVGs) have been around for a while, and understanding them is a great additional skill to have. "In the constant battle between high-resolution imagery and web performance concerns, there is pretty much only one way to go for logos, icons and illustrations on the web: SVG, " says Typekit's Jake Giltsoff. "Scalable Vector Graphics stay sharp at all screen resolutions, allow for very small file sizes, and can be easily edited, modified and maintained."

Using SVGs offers a number of benefits: reduced file sizes, improved performance, and the possibility of lean and efficient animations. These are all good things from a performance perspective.

User Experience Design

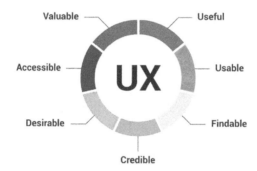

User experience (UX) design is the process of creating products that provide meaningful and relevant experiences to users. This involves the design of the entire process of acquiring and integrating the product, including aspects of branding, design, usability, and function.

"User Experience Design" is often used interchangeably with terms such as "User Interface Design" and "Usability". However, while Usability and User Interface Design are important aspects of UX Design, they are subsets of it – UX design covers a vast array of other areas, too. A UX designer is concerned with the *entire* process of acquiring and integrating a product, including aspects of branding, design, usability and function. It is a story that begins before the device is even in the user's hands.

> "No product is an island. A product is more than the product. It is a cohesive, integrated set of experiences. Think through all of the stages of a product or service – from initial intentions through final reflections, from first usage to help, service, and maintenance. Make them all work together seamlessly."

> — Don Norman, inventor of the term "User Experience"

Products that provide great user experience (e.g., the iPhone) are thus designed with not only the product's consumption or use in mind but also the entire process of acquiring, owning, and even troubleshooting it. Similarly, UX designers don't just focus on creating products that are usable; we concentrate on other aspects of the user experience, such as pleasure, efficiency and fun, too. Consequently, there is no single definition of a good user experience. Instead, a good user experience is one that meets a particular user's needs in the specific context where he or she uses the product.

UX Designers Consider the Why, What and How of Product Use

A UX designer will consider the Why, What and How of product use. The Why involves the users' motivations for adopting a product, whether they relate to a task they wish to perform with it, or to values and views associated with the ownership and use of the product. The addresses the things people can do with a product—its functionality. Finally, the How relates to the design of functionality in an accessible and aesthetically pleasant way. UX designers start with the Why before determining the What and then, finally, the How in order to create products that users can form meaningful experiences with. In software designs, designers must ensure the product's "substance" comes through an existing device and offers a seamless, fluid experience.

The Why, What and How of UX Design

UX Design is User-Centered

Since UX design encompasses the entire user journey, it's a multidisciplinary field – UX designers come from a variety of backgrounds such as visual design, programming, psychology and interaction design. Designing for human users also demands heightened scope regarding accessibility and accommodating many potential users' physical limitations, such as reading small text. A UX designer's typical tasks vary, but often include user research, creating personas, designing wireframes and interactive prototypes as well as testing designs. These tasks can vary greatly from one company to the next, but they always demand designers to be the users' advocate and keep the users' needs at the center of *all* design and development efforts. That's also why most UX designers work in some form of user-centered work process, and keep channeling their best-informed efforts until they address all of the relevant issues and user needs optimally.

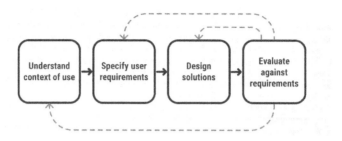

User-Centered Design is an iterative process that takes an understanding of the users and their context as a starting point for all design and development.

Situations that would Benefit from UX Design

Saying that all Web systems would benefit from a solid evaluation and design of the user experience is easy; arguing against it is hard if you care about user-centered design at all. But we don't live in a perfect world, and we don't have unlimited resources. Thus, we must prioritize and identify the areas that stand to gain the most from UX design and UX designers.

Complex Systems

The more complex the system, the more involved will the planning and architecture have to be for it. While investing in a full-blown multi-member UX study for a simple static website seems excessive, multi-faceted websites, interaction-rich Web applications and e-commerce websites stand to benefit a lot from UX design.

Systems that involve a myriad of user tasks must be perceived as being valuable, pleasant and efficient. Designers risk big losses in revenue by neglecting the user experience.

Start-Ups

Start-ups and smaller companies generally do not have the resources to hire dedicated employees for this. For example, 37Signals (now Basecamp), a lean start-up company that builds highly successful and robust Web applications, including Basecamp and Highrise, relies on well-rounded individuals, people who can "wear different hats."

In this situation, training existing employees (specifically, the Web designer) in the principles and processes of UX, or contracting out the UX work as needed, might be more suitable than hiring a full-time employee. However, creating a solid user experience for users in the very first versions of a product or service can certainly make it stand out and attract users' attention. But as the owner of a start-up, sometimes you may just not have enough resources for hiring a skilled UX designer.

Projects with "OK" Budgets

Smaller agencies that work for small and medium-sized businesses need to keep costs low for the customer base and prioritize deliverables in order to stay on the budget. The focus in these situations is more on the build process and less on planning, research and analysis. Projects with small budgets will be driven more by the launch of the final product. That doesn't mean that these projects wouldn't benefit from the good UX — of course they would — but in practice, small or medium-sized companies often do not feel compelled to invest resources into something that is not necessary for the launch of the site.

Projects with Longer Timeframes

By simple logic, adding a cog to the traditional website production process will extend the timeline. Time must be allotted for user experience design. UX designers could, in theory, shorten timelines by taking on some of the tasks traditionally assigned to Web designers and developers, thus potentially saving time and costs in revision phases by having addressed user issues.

Things To Know About UX Design

UX design is an amazing discipline, but it cannot, or will not, accomplish certain things.

UX Design Is Not One Size Fits All

User experience design won't work in every situation for every user because, as human beings, we are all different. What works for one person might have the opposite effect on another. The best we can do is design for specific experiences and promote certain behaviors, but we can't manufacture, impose or predict the actual experience itself.

And just as we can't design a user experience, we can't replicate the user experience for one website exactly on another website. User experiences will be different between websites. a design must be tailored to the goals, values, production process and products of its website.

Can't Be Directly Assessed With Traditional Metrics

You can't determine the effectiveness of a user experience design based solely on statistics such as page views, bounce rates and conversion rates. We can make assumptions, and we can ask users for anecdotal evidence, but we can't install an app (at least not yet) that automatically records user experience statistics directly.

Not the Same Thing as Usability

User experience and usability have become synonymous, but these two fields are clearly distinct. UX addresses how a user feels when using a system, while usability is about the user-friendliness and efficiency of the interface.

Usability is big part of the user experience and plays a major role in experiences that are effective and pleasant, but then human factors science, psychology, information architecture and user-centered design principles also play major roles.

Tasks And Techniques Of UX Designers

UX designers perform various tasks at various points in the process. Here are a few things that they deliver.

Evaluation of Current System

If a system already exists, a UX professional will holistically evaluate its current state. They will report issues and suggest fixes based on their analysis of research data.

A/B Testing

A UX specialist might devise a study to compare the effectiveness and quality of experience of different user interfaces.

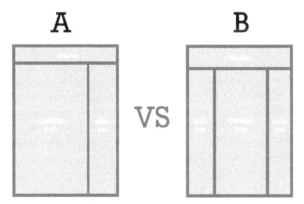

This is done by stating a hypothesis (e.g. "A green button is more attractive than a red button."), proposing or creating multiple versions of a design, defining what a "better experience" means (e.g. "The green button is better because users clicked it more.") and then conducting the test.

User Surveys

A UX designer could interview existing and potential users of the system to gain insight into what would be the most effective design. Because the user's experience is subjective, the best way to directly obtain information is by studying and interacting with users.

Wireframes and Prototypes

Based on their findings, UX specialists might develop wireframes of different layouts and perhaps also higher-fidelity prototypes.

User Flows

Designing how users should move through a system is another popular deliverable.

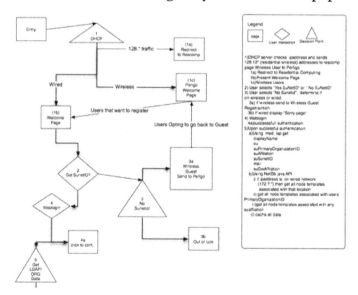

Storytelling

By engaging the emotions of users and drawing on familiar elements, UX designers tell stories and teach information.

Design Patterns

Patterns provide consistency and a way of finding the most effective "tool" for the job. With user interface design patterns, for example, picking the right UI elements (e.g.

module tabs, breadcrumbs, slideshows) for certain tasks based on their effectiveness leads to better and more familiar experiences. UX designers not only propose design patterns that are used on other websites, but develop custom patterns specifically for the current project.

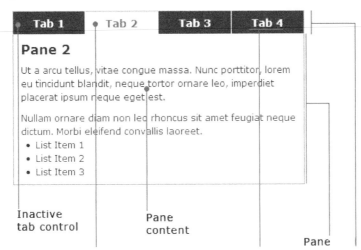

User Profiles and Personas

Knowing your audience is the first step in UX design and enables you to develop experiences that reflect the voice and emotions of your users. Personas can be developed using website data.

Content Inventory

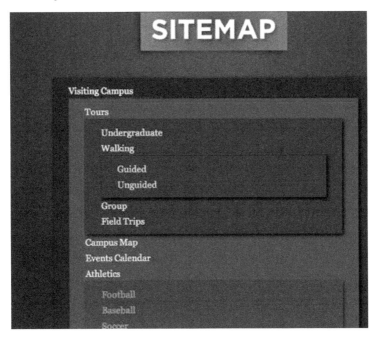

In the simplest of terms, content inventory is an organized list of pages on a website. Doing a content inventory is a step towards proposing changes in information architecture to enhance the user experience (e.g. user flow, findability and efficiency).

Content Style Guides

Consistency is critical to crafting a memorable user experience through your brand. Content style guides give writers and designers a framework in which to work when creating content and developing a design, and they also ensure that the brand and design elements align with the owner's goals.

Criticisms Of UX as a Profession

Not everyone sees the value of having a UX designer on the team. Arguments against hiring UX specialists revolve around the perceived associated costs, redundancy in skill set and fear of change.

Yet Another Thing to Worry About

The traditional website production process, especially at small agencies and start-ups, whose resources aren't as deep as they'd like, consists of one Web designer and one Web developer. The Web designer might be the one who develops the user experience, along with other tasks such as designing a wireframe and functional prototype, while the developer builds the production website as specified by the designer. A UX specialist only complicates this process.

Too Far Removed From the Process

A few people in the business of building websites believe that UX designers are too far removed from the actual process. Ryan Carson, founder of Carsonified and a leading voice in the Web design industry, for example, has criticized UX professionals who aren't "involved in the day-to-day process of designing, building, testing, marketing and updating a Web project."

This view of the profession basically says that UX professionals with no background in the actual process of building websites can't devise solutions as expertly as people who create the actual products.

However, many UX professionals do have a background in the build process; many were Web designers or developers who chose to specialize in this particular area of the production process.

Adds Expense

Simple logic dictates that hiring a UX person costs money (unless they're willing to work for free, and none are).

A counter-argument is that we should look at UX design as an investment. Although the benefits of UX are not as readily apparent as those of other parts of the website or application, it can lead to higher returns later on. For example, a simple improvement in the user experience design of a checkout process could increase revenue by millions of dollars.

Results are not Directly Measurable

Evaluating the effectiveness and return on investment of a UX design using quantitative measures is difficult. This is because the field is subjective. UX deals with users' emotions, and you can't put a number on it the way you can with page views, loading speed or conversion.

Instead, we have to tease out the results indirectly by analyzing revenue levels, page views, before-and-after surveys of users and the like. However, saying that any positive effects are the result of a better user experience or aesthetics or some other factor, such as improved marketing or front-end performance optimization, would be inconclusive.

The difficulty is in trying to quantify effects that are subjective in nature. We have to rely on qualitative evidence.

User Interface Design

User interface design is the discipline of designing software interfaces for devices, ideally with a focus on maximizing efficiency, responsiveness and aesthetics to foster a good user experience.

UI design is typically employed for products or services that require interaction for the user to get what they need from the experience. The interface should allow a user to perform any required tasks to complete the function of the product or service.

An interface is a point of interaction between the user and the hardware and/or software they are using. UI design is the skill employed to visualize the interface used to complete the task it is designed for. Good UI design facilitates making the completion of tasks as frictionless as possible and increasing usability.

A UI Designer is someone who creates the user interface based on a functional requirement and planned user experience using design standards and aesthetics to craft a certain experience.

UI Design can be done with pens and pencils, computer visualization software, or built directly in code or materials. The end results is an interface, or a simulation of one, that can be used to test, iterate and release a product or service.

User interface (UI) design focuses on anticipating what users might need to do and ensuring that the interface has elements that are easy to access, understand, and use to facilitate those actions. UI brings together concepts from interaction design, visual design, and information architecture.

Choosing Interface Elements

Users have become familiar with interface elements acting in a certain way, so try to be consistent and predictable in your choices and their layout. Doing so will help with task completion, efficiency, and satisfaction.

Interface elements include but are not limited to:

- Input Controls: buttons, text fields, checkboxes, radio buttons, dropdown lists, list boxes, toggles, date field

- Navigational Components: breadcrumb, slider, search field, pagination, slider, tags, icons

- Informational Components: tooltips, icons, progress bar, notifications, message boxes, modal windows

- Containers

There are times when multiple elements might be appropriate for displaying content. When this happens, it's important to consider the trade-offs. For example, sometimes elements that can help save you space, put more of a burden on the user mentally by forcing them to guess what is within the dropdown or what the element might be.

Best Practices for Designing an Interface

Everything stems from knowing your users, including understanding their goals, skills, preferences, and tendencies. Once you know about your user, make sure to consider the following when designing your interface:

- Keep the interface simple. The best interfaces are almost invisible to the user. They avoid unnecessary elements and are clear in the language they use on labels and in messaging.

- Create consistency and use common UI elements. By using common elements in your UI, users feel more comfortable and are able to get things done more quickly. It is also important to create patterns in language, layout and design throughout the site to help facilitate efficiency. Once a user learns how to do something, they should be able to transfer that skill to other parts of the site.

- Be purposeful in page layout. Consider the spatial relationships between items on the page and structure the page based on importance. Careful placement of items can help draw attention to the most important pieces of information and can aid scanning and readability.

- Strategically use color and texture. You can direct attention toward or redirect attention away from items using color, light, contrast, and texture to your advantage.

- Use typography to create hierarchy and clarity. Carefully consider how you use typeface. Different sizes, fonts, and arrangement of the text to help increase scanability, legibility and readability.

- Make sure that the system communicates what's happening. Always inform your users of location, actions, changes in state, or errors. The use of various UI elements to communicate status and, if necessary, next steps can reduce frustration for your user.

- Think about the defaults. By carefully thinking about and anticipating the goals people bring to your site, you can create defaults that reduce the burden on the user. This becomes particularly important when it comes to form design where you might have an opportunity to have some fields pre-chosen or filled out.

Flash

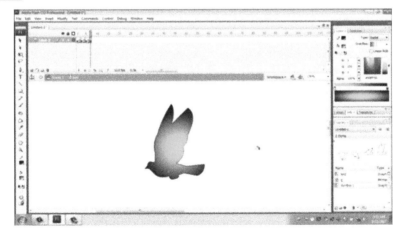

For websites, it is important to be seen and liked, for technologically, web designing has taken a big leap and made it easy to incorporate myriad features, thus, making it all about being attractive. Designers are in constant search to add newness to their websites and flash has come, as a great tool in that direction, for it is the software that adds dynamism to the website such that sound, light, and animation have become an integral part of the presentation on your website. Flash website design makes the virtual world come into reality.

The software 'Flash' can be used by any of the websites like games, information websites etc., as it helps to incorporate small details in the design and make it look real, a feature that catches the viewers' eye more. It also helps you to participate in moving the graphics that is so engrossing. The best examples are making your own music notes, playing games with sound more than your television sets. There are many things that you can do on your website with the help of Flash website design.

Website designers and developers who use flash to enrich the website help create a brand for the websites. They are designed to be uploaded fast in almost any bandwidth. The flash designs can help your e-business grow and be used for websites playing audios, videos, advertisement, etc. It can also be used for images or graphics that are still.

Reasons to Use Flash

- Cross-platform compatibility

  Flash is well-supported on something like 95-98% of the Web browsers out there, and if you build a site or application in Flash, you know that it will be viewed correctly by anyone who has the Flash plugin. It is operating system and browser independent.

- Animations

  Flash was originally used primarily as an animation tool, and that is what it is best suited for. It is easy to create animations in Flash, and then easy to view them.

- Video

  Video works well in Flash applications because it doesn't require an OS-dependent plugin like QuickTime or MediaPlayer.

- Games

  Games can be fun, and flash games don't have the browser support issues of Ajax the bandwidth limitations of server-side games written in CGI.

- Vector graphics

  Vector graphics can look smoother and more attractive and Flash allows developers to create applications with smooth lines requiring that the customer have a vector-graphic tool installed on their hard drive.

- Adds, well, flash to a site

- Image replacement for special fonts

  Web designers who need a special font family in their Web designs can use an image replacement technique called sIFR (or Scalable Inman Flash Replacement) which replaces text in the design with Flash to get specific fonts.

- Flash applications can perform script actions, collect data, and do most of the same things that server-side scripts can do.

- Drawbacks to Using Flash

- Bandwidth and Speed Limitations

  Unless the designer works very hard to optimize Flash most Flash applications and websites can be very large and slow to download. In many situations, the entire Flash site must be downloaded before it can be used. And while it is possible to add in graphical countdowns and other features to make the time pass more quickly, many people still won't wait.

- Usability is impaired

  One of the most important buttons on a Web browser is the back button. It is used all the time by most people browsing the Web. But a Flash site typically removes that functionality. When a customer hits the back button after delving deeply into a Flash site, s/he is taken back to the website they were on before they visited your site. Then if they return to your Flash site, they have to renavigate to where they were. Some people might be willing to do their work twice, but most won't.

- Accessibility is also impaired

  Because most Flash sites are based on images, and don't generally have a lot of alternative text, they can be very difficult or impossible for a screen reader to read.

- Search engines can't read them either

  Search engine spiders are a lot like screen readers, they can't parse images. Plus, many of them have trouble following links that are not standard HTML links - and most links in Flash are not in HTML - they are in Flash. Because of this, many Flash developers have a very difficult time getting their Flash sites to rank high in search engines. In fact, most Flash sites that do rank well, do so because they have two versions of the site - one Flash and one HTML. And then they have to maintain two copies of the same website.

- Flash requires a plug-in

  While a large proportion of Web browsers have the plug-in pre-installed, the fact is that Flash does require a plug-in which some people and companies don't allow.

- Some people just don't like Flash pages

  Similar to sound and animated graphics, Flash has developed a reputation among some customers as being more of an annoyance than a benefit to a Web page. This is especially true when the Flash serves no purpose other than to decorate a page - such as an animated banner or splash page. While these customers may be less common than those who don't care, they are often more vocal and more likely to sway opinion away from your site if you use Flash gratuitously.

Motion Graphics

Motion graphics is a new term for a specific genre of animation that been around for a while. Motion graphics are the crossroad between animation and graphic design. Usually, purpose-driven pieces with the goal of presenting information to the viewer through the use of animated text or graphics. They often have voice-overs narrating what the text or graphics are representing. Lyric videos are a nice example of motion graphics, the graphics echo what the singer is singing.

With the more widespread popularity and lower cost of computer animation, motion graphics began to differentiate themselves from regular animation. Motion graphics have begun to define a specific style as well. Often bright and colorful with no outlines (the lack of outlines makes the computer animation easier).

Fluid, Bouncy Animation Style

They usually are a very fluid, bouncy animation style. When you're working with narration you want to keep the viewer engaged visually so they don't just zone out and listen to the narrator. To do this motion graphics artists often make snazzy transitions and dynamic movement between text or between graphic images.

Motion graphics often tend to be more commercial and client driven. It's rare to see someone make an independent film in the style of a motion graphics piece. The reason for this has to do with the combination of graphic design and animation. Taking the commercial and client-based world of graphic design and combining it with animation ends up with motion graphics.

Motion graphics is not new however, it's just much easier to do now. Growing up we had a VHS tape called Donald Duck in Mathmagic Land. It did little to help us learn how to do math but it did contain motion graphics all the way back in 1959. The part where Donald plays pool (or billiards as they call it) where they show a representation of a pool table and draw the lines onto it is the same idea of motion graphics today.

They need to represent some information and illustrate an idea to the viewer so they do that through using animation and motion.

So why call it motion graphics instead of just simply referring to it as animation? Well, the cynical person in us says it's because everyone wants to be a special snowflake and have a neat sounding job title to impress people at parties.

Niche Artist Group

Motion graphics artists are trying to present themselves as a more niche artist group. Rather than the more broadly defined "animator" they choose to present themselves with the specific label of "motion graphics artist" just like how some people will say "character animator" rather than just simply animator. If you're an animator you could be a character animator, an abstract animator, any number of things. But by saying you're a motion graphics artist you let people know right away what you are and what you do.

Where it gets a little sticky is that the more popular the term motion graphics becomes it seems the more people are misaligning animations to it. Just because an animation is bright and colorful without outlines, like Alex Grigg's work, for example, doesn't mean it's motion graphics.

Reasons to Choose a Motion Graphics Video

1. Motion graphics is known for being one of the most sophisticated and elegant styles among marketing videos.

2. It's also one of the most formal styles among the different explainer video styles.

3. It gets the most out of visual designs and animations and can be used with an educational purpose, without losing its appeal.

4. It's one of the best styles to pass out numbers, stats and specific facts that could be harder to assimilate if you used any other style. This is due to its astonishing synthesis power.

5. It can turn the most boring and tedious information into the most appealing and enticing content.

Benefits Behind Motion Graphics

1. High Visual Power

Marketers generally resort to visuals to communicate their messages and ideas. Remember that we are all visual learners, this means that we understand concepts, assimilate and remember ideas with the help of drawings, diagrams, charts and different designs (visual content is highly enticing, attractive and also memorable). With this in mind, just imagine how effective video content can be, and even more so if we mixed it with graphics in motion. Motion graphics fits perfectly in this context and, as we're all visual learners, it helps you approach your target audience with persuasive, interesting and impressive content.

2. Stunning designs and animations

Motion graphics is not only about designs, but also about designs in motion. This means that motion graphics make use of animation techniques to make designs really come alive. With this type of video you can pass out any kind of idea by making use of graphic elements in movement. This will be of great help to deliver your message in just a couple of seconds, while you also make it understandable and memorable.

3. Getting to the perfect mix

This is a huge advantage that the motion graphics style offers: it can be merged with other explainer video styles so that you can maximize the benefits of both styles. What do we mean? Well, keep in mind that motion graphics can lack that human / emotional touch that other styles have. But if you need to give your video that special touch, you can consider adding some cute characters that trigger strong emotions in your audience, or even include a story behind all those figures and stats to make your story even more catchy. You have different possibilities when it comes to mixing styles, but we'll go over this later.

Different uses of the Motion Graphics Technique

1. Pass out a serious or professional image: if you sell a product or service that has a more "professional" profile, motion graphics is one of the best alternatives you can resort to in the video marketing arena.

2. Provide your video with an elegant style: remember that motion graphics is one of the most formal explainer video styles, so if you need to pass out an elegant and sophisticated image, pick this style.

3. Convey abstract concepts or ideas without losing "charm": motion graphics is perfect to pass out hard data, such as numbers, statistics, facts and any other information that could be harder to assimilate without making use of designs in motion.

4. Synthesize concepts and do it in an educational and cool way: just like an image is worth a thousand words, pictures in motion can have an astonishing power. By making use of motion graphics you can synthesize any idea, educate your audience, and do it in an attractive, interesting and catchy way.

5. Deliver your business idea effectively, specially if you have a B2B company, or a B2C company that is related to "hard data": if you have a software company, a financial company, or work with IT solutions, for instance, motion graphics is a great tool to deliver your business idea in a very straightforward and compelling way, without losing views.

Merging Motion Graphics with other Explainer Video Styles

It's not mandatory that your marketing video is "100% motion graphics". Remember that one of the best advantages of this technique is its versatility, so you can mix it with other styles to maximize the benefits of both worlds. In this sense, motion graphics can be merged with live action, character animation, or whiteboard animation.

Motion Graphics and Live Action

You may have heard that live action can have some limitations. But if you mix this technique with motion graphics, the limitations are only set by your imagination. With this combination you can transmit ideas or concepts that could be impossible to deliver by using Live Action only.

Motion Graphics with Character Animation

Remember that we said that motion graphics can lack that special human or personal touch that is typical of other explainer videos styles. If you need that warmer approach, then consider adding some charming and funny characters to your video. This way you will make it more "emotional" than a plain / standard motion graphics video.

Motion Graphics with whiteboard Animation

The motion graphics technique is part of every high quality whiteboard video, as it's used for the camera movements, the graphics, the hand animations and other elements. Most whiteboard videos are made digitally and motion graphics helps the elements look just great. So remember that in any high quality whiteboard video, there will be a motion graphics technique applied to it.

Website Builder

Website builder is an Internet-based website designing application that allows users to produce professional-looking website in very little time. With this, you can help your customers develop websites within minutes. An online website builder helps your customers obtain a fully functional online presence. Besides, updating the website's content or adding new content, images or multimedia content is easier via a user-friendly interface.

Uses of Website Builders

These systems are perfect for individuals, freelancers, photographers, small-time businesses and start-ups.

Website builder tool helps your customers build fully fledged websites quickly. Your customer can be charged on the basis of the Web Space and the number of web pages specified with a particular plan.

While conventional content management systems were designed to administer large websites, online website builders were designed keeping smaller website projects in mind. Essentially, the user doesn't require much of technical know-how or special programming skills like installing a CMS, applying a template, or creating a database.

This means that incorporating any changes to the website's design or templates is easier, while the content need not be modified in between.

Types of Website Builders

There are two main types of website builders: offline and online

1. Offline Website Builders

    Offline website builders come as software programs that you download and install on your computer. You will build your website and save your files on your computer, and when your website is ready, all you need to do is upload all your website files to a web host.

    One advantage of such website builders is that the software is running on your computer so you can work on your website even if you are offline. But because you will need to upload your files to a web host, you will need to have at least some technical skills or experience. You will also need to purchase a web hosting account in additional to the website builder software.

    Example of an offline website builder is Rapidweaver

2. Online Website Builders

    Online website builders are web-based and run on the provider's service. Unlike offline website builders, you don't need to download or install the software on your computer – all you need is a web browser (ie. Chrome, Firefox or Internet Explorer) and an Internet connection. This allows you to work on your website from anywhere and any device. Another benefit is that the website builder comes with web hosting services so you don't need to purchase it and/or set it up separately. Many online website builders are designed for people with little or no coding experience.

    Website.com is an example of an online website builder.

Anyone can use a website builder, but they're an especially good option for people who:

- Need to launch a website quickly.

- Don't have tech skills and don't have time or interest in learning.

- Feel intimidated by the idea of putting together their first website.

- Would rather let someone else handle site updates.

- Have a small site-design budget.

Because a good website builder will include templates for all types of use cases, bloggers, small business owners, and online retailers can all get professional looking sites up and running fast. For example, HostGator's website builder includes more than 100 templates for businesses such as restaurants, professional photography, and fashion and beauty retail, plus blog templates.

Working of Website Builders

First, you'll need a domain name for your site. If you've already registered your domain name, you're a step ahead. If not, the website builder should be able to help you get that done.

Next, you'll need a web hosting service, a place for your site's files to "live." Most website builders come packaged with one or more web hosting plans, so you can choose the level of service you need.

Now comes the fun part: putting together the elements you want from a menu of options.

- Templates. Go ahead and scroll through all your options a couple of times, and then narrow in on the designs that make the most sense for your type of website. If you run a business, you'll want a template that displays product photos on the home page, and if you're a blogger, you'll probably want a layout that makes it easy for visitors to scroll through your posts.

- Pages and sections. Even the most minimalist website needs a few standard pages and sections: the homepage, an "about us" page or section, contact information, and your content—blog posts, products, or a portfolio of your services. Business sites usually also include customer testimonials and reviews. And an FAQ section or page can save everyone time.

- Favicon. A whaticon? See the little Snappy on your browser tab at the top of this page? That's the HostGator favicon. You can create a similar custom image for your site, to make it easier for users to pick out your site when they have multiple tabs open, and to create a more appealing bookmark.

- E-commerce tools. If your site is your shop, you'll need to choose a shopping cart so customers can select your products, payment tools so they can checkout, and inventory management so you always know what's in stock, what's on backorder, and what's flying off your digital shelves.

- Images and video. Your website builder should have a library of high-quality images you can use to create headers and backgrounds. You should also be able to select tools to embed HD video. That will allow you to feature tutorial, product, and customer review videos on your site instead of having your visitors click away to watch them on YouTube.

- Social media. Want to share your thoughts, show off your merch, and drive traffic to your site? You'll be able to quickly link your social media accounts to your website. Site builder social media tools also make sharing from your site to your Facebook and other accounts a snap for you and your fans.

- SEO and analytics. Getting found and learning more about your site visitors is easy with built-in tools for search-engine optimization and Google analytics integration.

Pros and Cons of Website Builders

Using a website builder is fast, easy, and inexpensive. Those are some pretty impressive pros. But a website builder may not be the best choice if you need:

- Highly customized site code and functions.

- A fully customized template and theme.

- Dedicated servers to load your site at the highest possible speeds.

- Regular access to site backups.

If your site needs any of these elements, you may be better off using a CMS like WordPress or hiring a site designer and getting a dedicated hosting plan. For most site owners, though, a website builder will get the job done well.

References

- Introduction-to-web-design-3470022: lifewire.com, Retrieved 19 July 2018

- What-is-user-experience-design-overview-tools-and-resources: smashingmagazine.com, Retrieved 29 March 2018

- Flash-websites-pros-and-cons-3467364: thoughtco.com, Retrieved 16 April 2018

- 5-reasons-use-motion-graphics-video-wp: yumyumvideos.com, Retrieved 27 May 2018

- What-is-website-builder-how-does-website-builder-work, website-builder-and-web-design: website.com, Retrieved 30 June 2018

- What-is-a-website-builder: hostgator.com, Retrieved 10 April 2018

Web Programming

Web programming is the creation of dynamic web applications, for e-commerce sites, social networking sites, etc. The field of web programming has seen improved dynamic and interactive websites, due to an ever-growing set of technologies and tools. This chapter discusses in detail about asm.js, HTML5 audio, Opa, etc.

Asm.js

Asm.js comes from a new category of JavaScript application: C/C++ applications that've been compiled into JavaScript. It's a whole new genre of JavaScript application that's been spawned by Mozilla's Emscripten project.

Emscripten takes in C/C++ code, passes it through LLVM, and converts the LLVM-generated bytecode into JavaScript (specifically, Asm.js, a subset of JavaScript).

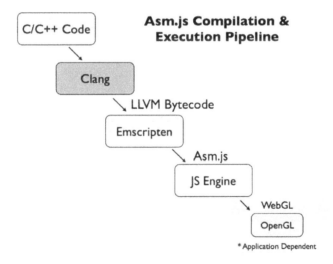

If the compiled Asm.js code is doing some rendering then it is most likely being handled by WebGL (and rendered using OpenGL). In this way the entire pipeline is technically making use of JavaScript and the browser but is almost entirely skirting the actual, normal, code execution and rendering path that JavaScript-in-a-webpage takes.

Asm.js is a subset of JavaScript that is heavily restricted in what it can do and how it can operate. This is done so that the compiled Asm.js code can run as fast as possible making as few assumptions as it can, converting the Asm.js code directly into assembly. It's important to note that Asm.js is just JavaScript – there is no special browser plugin or feature needed in order to make it work (although a browser that is able to detect and optimize Asm.js code will certainly run faster). It's a specialized subset of JavaScript that's optimized for performance, especially for this use case of applications compiled to JavaScript.

The best way to understand how Asm.js works, and its limitations, is to look at some Asm.js-compiled code. Let's look at a function extracted from a real-world Asm.js-compiled module (from the BananaBread demo). This code was formatted so that it'd be a little bit saner to digest – it's normally just a giant blob of heavily-minimized JavaScript:

```
function Vb(d) {
    d = d | 0;
    var e = 0, f = 0, h = 0, j = 0, k = 0, l = 0, m = 0, n = 0,
      o = 0, p = 0, q = 0, r = 0, s = 0;
    e = i;
    i = i + 12 | 0;
    f = e | 0;
    h = d + 12 | 0;
    j = c[h >> 2] | 0;
    if ((j | 0) > 0) {
      c[h >> 2] = 0;
      k = 0
    } else {
      k = j
    }
    j = d + 24 | 0;
    if ((c[j >> 2] | 0) > 0) {
      c[j >> 2] = 0
    }
    l = d + 28 | 0;
    c[l >> 2] = 0;
    c[l + 4 >> 2] = 0;
    l = (c[1384465] | 0) + 3 | 0;
    do {
      if (l >>> 0 < 26) {
        if ((4980736 >>> (l >>> 0) & 1 | 0) == 0) {
          break
        }
        if ((c[1356579] | 0) > 0) {
          m = d + 4 | 0;
          n = 0;
          while (1) {
            o = c[(c[1356577] | 0) + (n << 2) >> 2] | 0;
```

```
          do {
            if (a[o + 22 | 0] << 24 >> 24 == 24) {
              if (!(Vp(d, o | 0) | 0)) {
                break
              }
              p = (c[m >> 2] | 0) + (((c[h >> 2] | 0) - 1 | 0) * 40 & -1) +
12 | 0;
              q = o + 28 | 0;
              c[p >> 2] = c[q >> 2] | 0;
              c[p + 4 >> 2] = c[q + 4 >> 2] | 0;
              c[p + 8 >> 2] = c[q + 8 >> 2] | 0;
              c[p + 12 >> 2] = c[q + 12 >> 2] | 0;
              c[p + 16 >> 2] = c[q + 16 >> 2] | 0;
              c[p + 20 >> 2] = c[q + 20 >> 2] | 0;
              c[p + 24 >> 2] = c[q + 24 >> 2] | 0
            }
          } while (0);
          o = n + 1 | 0;
          if ((o | 0) < (c[1356579] | 0)) {
            n = o
          } else {
            break
          }
        }
        r = c[h >> 2] | 0
      } else {
        r = k
      } if ((r | 0) == 0) {
        i = e;
        return
      }
      n = c[j >> 2] | 0;
      if ((n | 0) >= 1) {
        i = e;
        return
      }
      m = f | 0;
      o = f + 4 | 0;
      q = f + 8 | 0;
      p = n;
      while (1) {
        g[m >> 2] = 0.0;
        g[o >> 2] = 0.0;
        g[q >> 2] = 0.0;
        Vq(d, p, f, 0, -1e3);
        n = c[j >> 2] | 0;
```

```
      if ((n | 0) < 1) {
        p = n
      } else {
        break
      }
    }
    i = e;
    return
  }
} while (0);
if ((c[1356579] | 0) <= 0) {
  i = e;
  return
}
f = d + 16 | 0;
r = 0;
while (1) {
  k = c[(c[1356577] | 0) + (r << 2) >> 2] | 0;
  do {
    if (a[k + 22 | 0] << 24 >> 24 == 30) {
      h = b[k + 14 >> 1] | 0;
      if ((h - 1 & 65535) > 1) {
        break
      }
      l = c[j >> 2] | 0;
      p = (c[1384465] | 0) + 3 | 0;
      if (p >>> 0 < 26) {
        s = (2293760 >>> (p >>> 0) & 1 | 0) != 0 ? 0 : -1e3
      } else {
        s = -1e3
      } if (!(Vq(d, l, k | 0, h << 16 >> 16, s) | 0)) {
        break
      }
      g[(c[f >> 2] | 0) + (l * 112 & -1) + 56 >> 2] = +(b[k + 12 >> 1] <<
16 >> 16 | 0);
      h = (c[f >> 2] | 0) + (l * 112 & -1) + 60 | 0;
      l = k + 28 | 0;
      c[h >> 2] = c[l >> 2] | 0;
      c[h + 4 >> 2] = c[l + 4 >> 2] | 0;
      c[h + 8 >> 2] = c[l + 8 >> 2] | 0;
      c[h + 12 >> 2] = c[l + 12 >> 2] | 0;
      c[h + 16 >> 2] = c[l + 16 >> 2] | 0;
      c[h + 20 >> 2] = c[l + 20 >> 2] | 0;
      c[h + 24 >> 2] = c[l + 24 >> 2] | 0
    }
```

```
    } while (0);
    k = r + 1 | 0;
    if ((k | 0) < (c[1356579] | 0)) {
      r = k
    } else {
      break
    }
  }
  i = e;
  return
}
```

Technically this is JavaScript code but we can already see that this looks nothing like most DOM-using JavaScript that we normally see. A few things we can notice just by looking at the code:

- This particular code only deals with numbers. In fact this is the case of all Asm. js code. Asm.js is only capable of handling a selection of different number types and no other data structure (this includes strings, booleans, or objects).

- All external data is stored and referenced from a single object, called the heap. Essentially this heap is a massive array (intended to be a typed array, which is highly optimized for performance). All data is stored within this array – effectively replacing global variables, data structures, closures, and any other forms of data storage.

- When accessing and setting variables the results are consistently coerced into a specific type. For example f = e | 0; sets the variable f to equal the value of e but it also ensures that the result will be an integer (| 0 does this, converting an value into an integer). We also see this happening with floats – note the use of 0.0 and g[...] = +(...).

- Looking at the values coming in and out of the data structures it appears as if the data structured represented by the variable c is an Int32Array (storing 32-bit integers, the values are always converted from or to an integer using | 0) and g is a Float32Array (storing 32-bit floats, the values always converted to a float by wrapping the value with +(...)).

By doing this the result is highly optimized and can be converted directly from this Asm.js syntax directly into assembly without having to interpret it, as one would normally have to do with JavaScript. It effectively shaves off a whole bunch of things that can make a dynamic language, like JavaScript, slow: Like the need for garbage collection and dynamic types.

As an example of some more-explanatory Asm.js code let's take a look at an example from the Asm.js specification:

```
function DiagModule(stdlib, foreign, heap) {
    "use asm";

    // Variable Declarations
    var sqrt = stdlib.Math.sqrt;

    // Function Declarations
    function square(x) {
        x = +x;
        return +(x*x);
    }

    function diag(x, y) {
        x = +x;
        y = +y;
        return +sqrt(square(x) + square(y));
    }

    return { diag: diag };
}
```

Looking at this module it seems downright understandable. Looking at this code we can better understand the structure of an Asm.js module. A module is contained within a function and starts with the "use asm"; directive at the top. This gives the interpreter the hint that everything inside the function should be handled as Asm.js and be compiled to assembly directly.

Note, at the top of the function, the three arguments: stdlib, foreign, and heap. The stdlib object contains references to a number of built-in math functions. foreign provides access to custom user-defined functionality (such as drawing a shape in WebGL). And finally heap gives you an ArrayBuffer which can be viewed through a number of different lenses, such as Int32Array and Float32Array.

The rest of the module is broken up into three parts: variable declarations, function declarations, and finally an object exporting the functions to expose to the user.

The export is an especially important point to understand as it allows all of the code within the module to be handled as Asm.js but still be made usable to other, normal, JavaScript code. Thus you could, theoretically, have some code that looks like the following, using the above DiagModule code:

```
document.body.onclick = function() {
    function DiagModule(stdlib){"use asm"; ... return { ... };}

    var diag = DiagModule({ Math: Math }).diag;
    alert(diag(10, 100));
};
```

This would result in an Asm.js DiagModule that's handled special by the JavaScript interpreter but still made available to other JavaScript code (thus we could still access it and use it within a click handler, for example).

Performance of Asm.js

Right now the only implementation that exists is in nightly versions of Firefox (and even then, for only a couple platforms). That being said early numbers show the performance being *really, really* good. For complex applications (such as the above games) performance is only around 2x slower than normally-compiled C++ (which is comparable to other languages like Java or C#). This is substantially faster than current browser runtimes, yielding performance that's about 4-10x faster than the latest Firefox and Chrome builds.

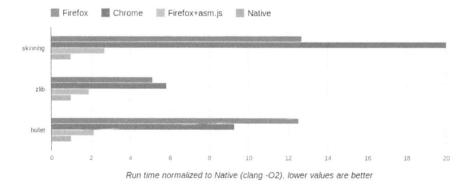

Run time normalized to Native (clang -O2), lower values are better

This is a substantial improvement over the current best case. Considering how early on in the development of Asm.js is it's very likely that there could be even greater performance improvements coming.

It is interesting to see such a large performance chasm appearing between Asm.js and the current engines in Firefox and Chrome. A 4-10x performance difference is substantial (this is in the realm of comparing these browsers to the performance of IE 6). Interestingly even with this performance difference many of these Asm.

js demos are still usable on Chrome and Firefox, which is a good indicator for the current state of JavaScript engines. That being said their performance is simply not as good as the performance offered by a browser that is capable of optimizing Asm. js code.

Use Cases

It should be noted that almost all of the applications that are targeting Asm.js right now are C/C++ applications compiled to Asm.js using Emscripten. With that in mind the kind of applications that are going to target Asm.js, in the near future, are those that will benefit from the portability of running in a browser but which have a level of complexity in which a direct port to JavaScript would be infeasible.

So far most of the use cases have centered around code bases where performance is of the utmost importance: Such as in running games, graphics, programming language interpreters, and libraries. A quick look through the Emscripten project list shows many projects which will be of instant use to many developers.

- A number of game engines have already been ported. A good demo of what is possible is the BananaBread FPS Game (Source Code) which is playable directly in the browser and features multiplayer and bots.

- A port of LaTeX to JavaScript, called texlive.js, using Emscripten, allowing you to compile PDFs completely within your browser.

- A port of SQLite to JavaScript capable of running in Node.js.

- NaCL: A Networking and Cryptography Library

Asm.js Support

The nightly version of Firefox is currently the only browser that supports optimizing Asm.js code.

However it's important to emphasize that Asm.js-formatted JavaScript code is still just JavaScript code, albeit with an important set of restrictions. For this reason Asm. js-compiled code can still run in other browsers as normal JavaScript code, even if that browser doesn't support it.

The critical puzzle piece is the performance of that code: If a browser doesn't support typed arrays or doesn't specially-compile the Asm.js code then the performance is going to be much worse off. Of course this isn't special to Asm.js, likely any browser that doesn't have those features is also suffering in other ways.

Asm.js and Web Development

As you can probably see from the code above Asm.js isn't designed to be written by hand. It's going to require some sort of tooling to write and it's going to require some rather drastic changes from how one would normally write JavaScript, in order to use. The most common use case for Asm.js right now is in applications complied from C/C++ to JavaScript. Almost none of these applications interact with the DOM in a meaningful way, beyond using WebGL and the like.

In order for it to be usable by regular developers there are going to have to be some intermediary languages that are more user-accessible that can compile to Asm.js. The best candidate, at the moment, is LLJS in which work is starting to get it compiling to Asm.js. It should be noted that a language like LLJS is still going to be quite different from regular JavaScript and will likely confuse many JavaScript users. Even with a nice more-user-accessible language like LLJS it's likely that it'll still only be used by hard-core developers who want to optimize extremely complex pieces of code.

Even with LLJS, or some other language, that could allow for more hand-written Asm. js code we still wouldn't have an equally-optimized DOM to work with. The ideal environment would be one where we could compile LLJS code and the DOM together to create a single Asm.js blob which could be executed simultaneously.

HTML5 Audio

HTML5 features include native audio support without the need for Flash.

Embedding Audio in HTML Document

Inserting sound onto a web page is not relatively easy, because browsers did not have a uniform standard for defining embedded media files.

Using the HTML5 audio Element

The newly introduced HTML5 <audio> element provides a standard way to embed audio in web pages. However, the audio element is relatively new, but it works in most of the modern web browsers. The following example simply inserts an audio into the HTML5 document, using the browser default set of controls, with one source.

Example
```
1. <audio controls="controls" src="birds.mp3">
2.     Your browser does not support the HTML5 Audio element.
3. </audio>
```

An audio, using the browser default set of controls, with alternative sources.

Example

```
1.  <audio controls="controls">
2.      <source src="birds.mp3" type="audio/mpeg">
3.      <source src="birds.ogg" type="audio/ogg">
4.      Your browser does not support the HTML5 Audio element.
5.  </audio>
```

The 'ogg' track in the above example works in Firefox, Opera and Chrome, while the same track in the 'mp3' format is added to make the audio work in Internet Explorer and Safari.

Linking Audio Files

You can make links to your audio files and pay it by ticking on them.

Example

```
1.  <a href="sea.mp3">Track 1</a>
2.  <a href="wind.mp3">Track 2</a>
```

Using the Object Element

The <object> element is used to embed different kinds of media files into an HTML document. Initially, this element was used to insert ActiveX controls, but according to the specification, an object can be any media object such as video, audio, Java applets, ActiveX, document (HTML, PDF, Word, etc.), Flash animations or even images. Here's an example:

Example

```
1.  <object data="sea.mp3" width="200px" height="50px"></object>
2.  <object data="sea.ogg" width="200px" height="50px"></object>
```

Warning: The <object> element is not supported widely and very much depends on the type of the object that's being embedded. Other methods like HTML5 <audio> element or Google MP3 player could be a better choice in many cases.

JavaScript

JavaScript is a scripting or programming language that allows you to implement complex things on web pages — every time a web page does more than just sit there and display static information for you to look at — displaying timely content updates, interactive maps, animated 2D/3D graphics, scrolling video jukeboxes, etc. — you can bet that JavaScript is probably involved. It is the third layer of the layer cake of standard web technologies, two of which (HTML and CSS) we have covered in much more detail in other parts of the Learning Area.

Let's take a simple text label as an example. We can mark it up using HTML to give it structure and purpose:

```
1 <p>Player 1: Chris</p>
```

Player 1: Chris

Then we can add some CSS into the mix to get it looking nice:

```
1 p {
2 font-family: 'helvetica neue', helvetica, sans-serif;
3 letter-spacing: 1px;
4 text-transform: uppercase;
5 text-align: center;
6 border: 2px solid rgba(0,0,200,0.6);
7 background: rgba(0,0,200,0.3);
8 color: rgba(0,0,200,0.6);
9 box-shadow: 1px 1px 2px rgba(0,0,200,0.4);
10 border-radius: 10px;
11 padding: 3px 10px;
12 display: inline-block;
```

```
13 cursor: pointer;

14 }
```

Player 1: Chris

And finally, we can add some JavaScript to implement dynamic behaviour:

```
1 var para = document.querySelector('p');

2 para.addEventListener('click', updateName);

3 function updateName() {
4 var name = prompt('Enter a new name');
5 para.textContent = 'Player 1: ' + name;
6 }
```

Programming features of JavaScript

The core JavaScript language consists of some common programming features that allow you to do things like:

- Store useful values inside variables. In the above example for instance, we ask for a new name to be entered then store that name in a variable called name.

- Operations on pieces of text (known as "strings" in programming). In the above example we take the string "Player 1: " and join it to the name variable to create the complete text label, e.g. "Player 1: Chris".

- Running code in response to certain events occurring on a web page. We used a click event in our example above to detect when the button is clicked and then run the code that updates the text label.

- And much more.

What is even more exciting however is the functionality built on top of the core JavaScript language. So-called Application Programming Interfaces (APIs) provide you with extra superpowers to use in your JavaScript code.

APIs are ready-made sets of code building blocks that allow a developer to implement programs that would otherwise be hard or impossible to implement. They do the same thing for programming that ready-made furniture kits do for home building — it is much easier to take ready-cut panels and screw them together to make a bookshelf than it is to work out the design yourself, go and find the correct wood, cut all the panels to the right size and shape, find the correct-sized screws, and *then* put them together to make a bookshelf.

They generally fall into two categories:

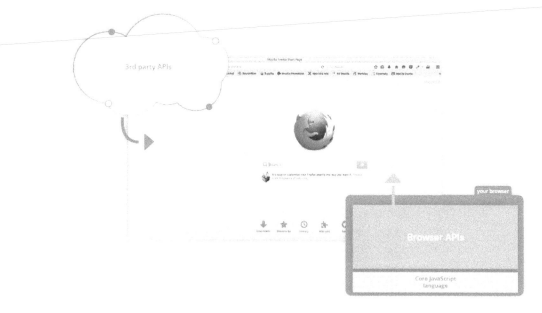

Browser APIs are built into your web browser, and are able to expose data from the surrounding computer environment, or do useful complex things. For example:

- The DOM (Document Object Model) API allows you to manipulate HTML and CSS, creating, removing and changing HTML, dynamically applying new styles to your page, etc. Everytime you see a popup window appear on a page, or some new content displayed (as we saw above in our simple demo) for example, that's the DOM in action.

- The Geolocation API retrieves geographical information. This is how Google Maps is able to find your location, and plot it on a map.

- The Canvas and WebGL APIs allow you to create animated 2D and 3D graphics. People are doing some amazing things using these web technologies —see Chrome Experiments and webglsamples.

- Audio and Video APIs like HTMLMediaElement and WebRTC allow you to do really interesting things with multimedia, such as play audio and video right in a web page, or grab video from your web camera and display it on someone else's computer.

Third party APIs are not built into the browser by default, and you generally have to grab their code and information from somewhere on the Web. For example:

- The Twitter API allows you to do things like displaying your latest tweets on your website.

- The Google Maps API allows you to embed custom maps into your website, and other such functionality.

We'll start actually looking at some code, and while doing so explore what actually happens when you run some JavaScript in your page.

Let's briefly recap the story of what happens when you load a web page in a browser. When you load a web page in your browser, you are running your code (the HTML, CSS, and JavaScript) inside an execution environment (the browser tab). This is like a factory that takes in raw materials (the code) and outputs a product (the web page).

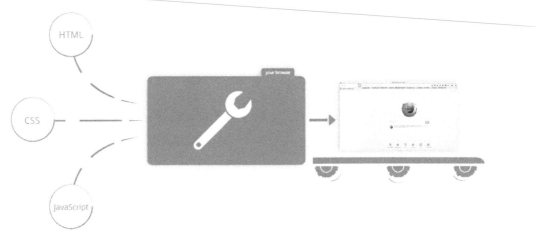

The JavaScript is executed by the browser's JavaScript engine, after the HTML and CSS have been assembled and put together into a web page. This ensures that the structure and style of the page are already in place by the time the JavaScript starts to run.

This is a good thing, as a very common use of JavaScript is to dynamically modify HTML and CSS to update a user interface, via the Document Object Model API (as mentioned above). If the JavaScript loaded and tried to run before the HTML and CSS were there to affect, then errors would occur.

Browser Security

Each browser tab is its own separate bucket for running code in (these buckets are called "execution environments" in technical terms) — this means that in most cases the code in each tab is run completely separately, and the code in one tab cannot directly affect the code in another tab — or on another website. This is a good security measure — if this were not the case, then pirates could start writing code to steal information from other websites, and other such bad things.

JavaScript Running Order

When the browser encounters a block of JavaScript, it generally runs it in order, from top to bottom. This means that you need to be careful what order you put things in. For example, let's return to the block of JavaScript we saw in our first example:

```
1 var para = document.querySelector('p');

2

3 para.addEventListener('click', updateName);

4

5 function updateName() {

6 var name = prompt('Enter a new name');

7 para.textContent = 'Player 1: ' + name;

8 }
```

Here we are selecting a text paragraph (line 1), then attaching an event listener to it (line 3) so that when the paragraph is clicked, the updateName() code block (lines 5–8) is run. The updateName() code block (these types of reusable code blocks are called "functions") asks the user for a new name, and then inserts that name into the paragraph to update the display.

If you swapped the order of the first two lines of code, it would no longer work — instead, you'd get an error returned in the browser developer console — TypeError: para is undefined. This means that the para object does not exist yet, so we can't add an event listener to it.

Interpreted versus Compiled Code

You might hear the terms interpreted and compiled in the context of programming. In interpreted languages, the code is run from top to bottom and the result of running the code is immediately returned. You don't have to transform the code into a different form before the browser runs it.

Compiled languages on the other hand are transformed (compiled) into another form before they are run by the computer. For example C/C++ are compiled into assembly language that is then run by the computer.

JavaScript is a lightweight interpreted programming language. Both approaches have different advantages.

Server-side versus Client-side Code

You might also hear the terms server-side and client-side code, especially in the context of web development. Client-side code is code that is run on the user's computer — when a web page is viewed, the page's client-side code is downloaded, then run and displayed by the browser.

Server-side code on the other hand is run on the server, then its results are downloaded and displayed in the browser. Examples of popular server-side web languages include PHP, Python, Ruby, and ASP.NET. And JavaScript! JavaScript can also be used as a server-side language, for example in the popular Node.js environment.

Dynamic versus Static Code

The word dynamic is used to describe both client-side JavaScript, and server-side languages — it refers to the ability to update the display of a web page/app to show different things in different circumstances, generating new content as required. Server-side code dynamically generates new content on the server, e.g. pulling data from a database, whereas client-side JavaScript dynamically generates new content inside the browser on the client, e.g. creating a new HTML table, filling it with data requested from the server, then displaying the table in a web page shown to the user. The meaning is slightly different in the two contexts, but related, and both approaches (server-side and client-side) usually work together.

A web page with no dynamically updating content is referred to as static — it just shows the same content all the time.

Adding JavaScript to your Page

JavaScript is applied to your HTML page in a similar manner to CSS. Whereas CSS uses <link> elements to apply external stylesheets and <style> elements to apply internal stylesheets to HTML, JavaScript only needs one friend in the world of HTML — the <script> element. Let's learn how this works.

Internal JavaScript

1. First of all, make a local copy of our example file apply-javascript.html. Save it in a directory somewhere sensible.

2. Open the file in your web browser and in your text editor. You'll see that the HTML creates a simple web page containing a clickable button.

3. Next, go to your text editor and add the following in your head — just before your closing </head> tag:

```
1 <script>
```

```
2

3   // JavaScript goes here

4

5  </script>
```

4. Now we'll add some JavaScript inside our <script> element to make the page do something more interesting — add the following code just below the "// JavaScript goes here" line:

```
1 document.addEventListener("DOMContentLoaded", function() {

2   function createParagraph() {

3     var para = document.createElement('p');

4     para.textContent = 'You clicked the button!';

5     document.body.appendChild(para);

6   }

7

8   var buttons = document.querySelectorAll('button');

9

10    for(var i = 0; i < buttons.length ; i++) {

11      buttons[i].addEventListener('click', createParagraph);

12    }

13 });
```

5. Save your file and refresh the browser — now you should see that when you click the button, a new paragraph is generated and placed below.

External JavaScript

This works great, but what if we wanted to put our JavaScript in an external file? Let's explore this now.

1. First, create a new file in the same directory as your sample HTML file. Call it script.js — make sure it has that .js filename extension, as that's how it is recognized as JavaScript.

2. Replace your current <script> element with the following:

```
1 <script src="script.js" defer></script>
```

3. Inside script.js, add the following script:

```
1 function createParagraph() {
```

```
2    var para = document.createElement('p');

3    para.textContent = 'You clicked the button!';

4    document.body.appendChild(para);

5 }

6

7 var buttons = document.querySelectorAll('button');

8

9 for(var i = 0; i < buttons.length ; i++) {

10    buttons[i].addEventListener('click', createParagraph);

11 }
```

4. Save and refresh your browser, and you should see the same thing! It works just the same, but now we've got our JavaScript in an external file. This is generally a good thing in terms of organizing your code, and making it reusable across multiple HTML files. Plus the HTML is easier to read without huge chunks of script dumped in it.

Inline JavaScript Handlers

Note that sometimes you'll come across bits of actual JavaScript code living inside HTML. It might look something like this:

```
1 function createParagraph() {

2 var para = document.createElement('p');

3 para.textContent = 'You clicked the button!';

4 document.body.appendChild(para);

5 }
```

```
1 <button onclick="createParagraph()">Click me!</button>
```

Using a pure JavaScript construct allows you to select all the buttons using one instruction. The code we used above to serve this purpose looks like this:

```
1 var buttons = document.querySelectorAll('button');

2

3 for (var i = 0; i < buttons.length ; i++) {

4 buttons[i].addEventListener('click', createParagraph);

5 }
```

This might be a bit longer than the onclick attribute, but it will work for all buttons — no matter how many are on the page, nor how many are added or removed. The JavaScript does not need to be changed.

Script Loading Strategies

There are a number of issues involved with getting scripts to load at the right time. Nothing is as simple as it seems. A common problem is that all the HTML on a page is loaded in the order in which it appears. If you are using JavaScript to manipulate elements on the page (or more accurately, the Document Object Model), your code won't work if the JavaScript is loaded and parsed before the HTML you are trying to do something to.

In the above code examples, in the internal and external examples the JavaScript is loaded and run in the head of the document, before the HTML body is parsed. This could cause an error, so we've used some constructs to get around it.

In the internal example, you can see this structure around the code:

```
1 document.addEventListener("DOMContentLoaded", function() {
2 ...
3 });
```

This is an event listener, which listens for the browser's "DOMContentLoaded" event, which signifies that the HTML body is completely loaded and parsed. The JavaScript inside this block will not run until after that event is fired, therefore the error is avoided.

In the external example, we use a more modern JavaScript feature to solve the problem, the async attribute, which tells the browser to continue downloading the HTML content once the <script> tag element has been reached.

```
1 <script src="script.js" async></script>
```

In this case both the script and the HTML will load simultaneously and the code will work.

An old-fashioned solution to this problem used to be to put your script element right at the bottom of the body (e.g. just before the </body> tag), so that it would load after all the HTML has been parsed. The problem with this solution is that loading/parsing of the script is completely blocked until the HTML DOM has been loaded. On larger sites with lots of JavaScript, this can cause a major performance issue, slowing down your site. This is why async was added to browsers.

Async and Defer

There are actually two ways we can bypass the problem of the blocking script — async and defer. Let's look at the difference between these two.

Async scripts will download the script without blocking rendering the page and will execute it as soon as the script finishes downloading. You get no guarantee that scripts will run in any specific order, only that they will not stop the rest of the page from displaying. It is best to use async when the scripts in the page run independently from each other and depend on no other script on the page.

For example, if you have the following script elements:

```
1 <script async src="js/vendor/jquery.js"></script>
2
3 <script async src="js/script2.js"></script>
4
5 <script async src="js/script3.js"></script>
```

You can't rely on the order the scripts will load in. jquery.js may load before or after script2.js and script3.js and if this is the case, any functions in those scripts depending on jquery will produce an error because jquery will not be defined at the time the script runs.

Defer will run the scripts in the order they appear in the page and execute them as soon as the script and content are downloaded:

```
1 <script defer src="js/vendor/jquery.js"></script>
2
3 <script defer src="js/script2.js"></script>
4
5 <script defer src="js/script3.js"></script>
```

All the scripts with the defer attribute will load in the order they appear on the page. So in the second example, we can be sure that jquery.js will load before script2.js and script3.js and that script2.js will load before script3.js.

To summarize:

- If your scripts can run independently without dependencies then use async.

- If your scripts depend on other scripts load them using defer and put their corresponding <script> elements in the order you want the browser to execute them.

Comments

As with HTML and CSS, it is possible to write comments into your JavaScript code that will be ignored by the browser, and exist simply to provide instructions to your fellow developers on how the code works (and you, if you come back to your code after six months and can't remember what you did). Comments are very useful, and you should use them often, particularly for larger applications. There are two types:

- A single line comment is written after a double forward slash (//), e.g.

```
1 // I am a comment
```

- A multi-line comment is written between the strings /* and */, e.g.

```
1 /*
2    I am also
3    a comment
4 */
```

So for example, we could annotate our last demo's JavaScript with comments like so:

```
1 // Function: creates a new paragraph and append it to the bottom
    of the HTML body.
2
3 function createParagraph() {
4 var para = document.createElement('p');
5 para.textContent = 'You clicked the button!';
6 document.body.appendChild(para);
7 }
8
9 /*
10   1. Get references to all the buttons on the page and sort them
    in an array.
11   2. Loop through all the buttons and add a click event listener
    to each one.
12
13 When any button is pressed, the createParagraph() function will be run.
14 */
15
16 var buttons = document.querySelectorAll('button');
17
18 for (var i = 0; i < buttons.length ; i++) {
19 buttons[i].addEventListener('click', createParagraph);
20 }
```

Opa

```
hello.opa

1    import stdlib.themes.bootstrap
2    database int /counter = 0;
3    function action(_) {
4        /counter++;
5        #msg = <div>Thank you, user number {/counter}!</div>
6    }
7    function page() {
8        <h1 id="msg">Hello</h1>
9        <a class="btn" onclick={action}>Click me</a>
10   }
11   Server.start(
12       Server.http,
13       { ~page, title: "Database Demo" }
14   )

Line 14, Column 2                          Tab Size: 4        Opa
```

Opa is a full-stack open source web development framework for JavaScript that lets you write *secure* and *scalable* web applications.

Opa generates standard Node.js/MongoDB applications, natively supports HTML5 and CSS and automates many aspects of modern web application programming: Ajax/ Comet client-server communication, event-driven and non-blocking programming models.

Opa enables to write full-stack applications:

- *Server* (backend) programming (running on node.Js),
- *Client* (frontend) programming (compiled to javascript) and
- *Database* programming (using MongoDB).

Full-stack

Opa handles all aspects of web programming: frontend (client code), backend (server code) and database queries are all written in one consistent language and compiled to standards of the web: JavaScript frontend, Node.js backend and MongoDB for the database. Other targets are planned, making Opa a gateway to web programming.

You can write a complete Opa program without thinking about the client-server distinction and the Opa compiler will distribute the code as needed for you and take care of all the communication. Should you need to tweak the choices made by the compiler (for instance to improve the application performance) it's very easy with simple keywords like client, server and more for fine-tuning.

```
// Opa decides

function client_or_server(x, y) { ... }
```

```
// Client-side
client function client_function(x, y) { ... }
// Server-side
server function server_function(x, y) { ... }
```

The database code can also be written directly in Opa. Opa supports the major NoSQL databases: CouchDB and MongoDB. The latter requires no configuration at all and is recommended for beginners, while the former offers state-of-the-art reliability and performance.

Easy Workflow

To write an application, first type the code in your favorite editor. The simplest "Hello, world" application in Opa is written in just a few lines:

```
Server.start(
    Server.http,
    { title: "Hello, world"
    , page: function() { <h1>Hello, world</h1> }
    }
)
```

The program can be compiled and run with the following single command line: opa hello.opa --

Familiar Syntax

Opa syntax is inspired by popular programming languages, most notably, JavaScript. Below is an extract of a real Opa program:

```
function createUser(username, password) {
        match (findUser(username)) {
        case {none}:
          user =
            { username: username
            , fullname: ""
```

```
      , password: Crypto.Hash.sha2(password)
      };
    saveUser(user);
  default:
    displayMessage("This username exists");
  };
  Client.goto("/login");
}
```

Opa however extends the classical syntax with advanced features specific to the web. HTML fragments can be inserted directly without quotes: line = <div id="foo">bar</div>;

CSS selectors readily available: selector = #foo;

And a pointer-like syntax allows to apply a given content to a selector: *selector = line;

Opa provides event-driven programming. For instance, running a function when an event is triggered is accomplished in the following way:

```
function action(event) {
  #foo = <div id="bar" />;
}
...
<div onclick={action} />
```

Static Typing

One of the most important features of Opa is its typing system. Although Opa may look like and has many advantages of dynamic programming languages, it is a compiled language which relies on a state-of-the-art type system.

Opa checks the types at compile time, which means that no type error can happen at runtime. For instance, the following code foo = 1 + "bar"; raises the following error at compile time:

```
Type Conflict
  (1:7-1:7)              int
  (1:11-1:15)            string


  The types of the first argument and the second argument
    of function + of stdlib.core should be the same
```

Unlike C or Java, you don't have to annotate types yourself as Opa features almost complete type inference. For instance, you can just write:

```
function foo(s) {
    String.length(s);
}
function bar(x, y) {
    foo(x) + y;
}
```

and the Opa compilers automatically infers the types, as if you've written:

```
int function foo(string s) {
    String.length(s);
}
int function bar(string x, int y) {
    foo(x) + y;
}
```

This system will become your wingman while you code. For instance, we will present four types of errors that are caught at compile time.

If you write:

```
element =
  <div>
    <span>{prompt({none})}</span>
    <span>{expr}
  </div>
  <div>{Calc.compute(expr)}</div>;
```

The compiler will tell you that there is an *"Open and close tag mismatch ,found at (48:8-48:11), vs ."*.

If you write:

```
case {some: 13}: #status = "Enter"; callback(get());
case {some: 37}: #status = "Left"; move({lef});
case {some: 38}: #status = "Up"; move({up});
case {some: 39}: #status = "Right"; move({right});
```

The compiler will tell you that the type of this function is not right. *You are using a type { lef } when a type { left } or { right } or { rightmost } or { up } or { down } is expected.* The latter type is not declared anywhere in the code, but rather was inferred by the Opa compiler from the rest of the code.

If you write:

```
previous = Dom.get_content(#precaret);

#precaret = String.sub(0, String.lenght(previous) - 1, previous);

#postcaret += String.get(String.length(previous) - 1, previous);
```

the compiler will tell you that String module has no lenght function and will suggest that maybe you meant length or init instead?

If you write:

```
previous = Dom.get_content(#postcaret);

#postcaret = String.sub(1, String.length(previous) - 1, previous);

#precaret =+ String.get(previous);
```

the compiler will tell you that String.get takes 2 arguments, but only 1 is given. And will suggest that the 1st-argument is of type int.

Opa type system not only manages basic types but complex data-structures, functions and even modules!

Database

Opa has extensive support for MongoDB (and, to lesser extent, CouchDB) offering a state-of-the-art solution for data storage and retrieval.

Database values are declared by stating their type: database type /path; for instance database int /counter;

In the line above, /counter is called a *path*, as accessing stored values bears similarities to browsing a filesystem. Getting a value from the database is simply accomplished with: /counter while storing (or replacing) a value with: /path <- value

You can store complex datastructures in the database, like maps. A map is a datastructure that associates a value to each key. The path system recognize such datastructures and allows to specify a key directly in the path. For instance, you can write:

```
database stringmap(string) /dictionary;

...

/dictionary[key];

...
```

```
/dictionary[key] <- value;

...
```

Opa offers scaffolding for easy project creation. Just write opa create myapp

This will create a skeleton of a new app named myapp based on the MVC architecture. Run it with:

```
cd myapp

make run
```

Edit the sources in the src and resources in the resources directory. You can also try opa create --help for more options.

Web Components

Web components are a set of web platform APIs that allow you to create new custom, re-usable, encapsulated HTML tags to use in web pages and web apps. Custom components and widgets build on the Web Component standards, will work across modern browsers, and can be used with any JavaScript library or framework that works with HTML.

Web components are based on existing web standards. Features to support web components are currently being added to the HTML and DOM specs, letting web developers easily extend HTML with new elements with encapsulated styling and custom behavior.

Specifications

Web components are based on four main specifications:

Custom Elements

The Custom Elements specification lays the foundation for designing and using new types of DOM elements.

Shadow DOM

The shadow DOM specification defines how to use encapsulated style and markup in web components.

ES Modules

The ES Modules specification defines the inclusion and reuse of JS documents in a standards based, modular, performant way.

HTML Template

The HTML template element specification defines how to declare fragments of markup that go unused at page load, but can be instantiated later on at runtime.

Using a Web Component

The components on this site provide new HTML elements that you can use in your web pages and web applications.

Using a custom element is as simple as importing it, and using the new tags in an HTML document. For example, to use the paper-button element:

```
<script type="module" href="node_modules/@polymer/paper-button/pa-
    per-button.js"></script>

. . .

<paper-button raised class="indigo">raised</paper-button>
```

There are a number of ways to install custom elements. When you find an element you want to use, look at its README for the commands to install it. Most elements today can be installed with NPM. NPM also handles installing the components' dependencies.

For example, the paper-button overview describes the install process with npm:

```
mkdir my-new-app && cd my-new-app
npm install --save @polymer/paper-button
```

Defining a New HTML element

This part describes the syntax for the cross-browser version of the web components specification.

Use JavaScript to define a new HTML element and its tag with the customElements global. Call customElements.define() with the tag name you want to create and a JavaScript class that extends the base HTMLElement.

For example, to define a mobile drawer panel, <app-drawer>:

```
class AppDrawer extends HTMLElement {...}
window.customElements.define('app-drawer', AppDrawer);
```

To use the new tag:

```
<app-drawer></app-drawer>
```

Using a custom element is no different to using a <div> or any other element. Instances can be declared on the page, created dynamically in JavaScript, event listeners can be attached, etc.

```
<script>
// Create with javascript
var newDrawer = document.createElement('app-drawer');
// Add it to the page
document.body.appendChild(newDrawer);
// Attach event listeners
document.querySelector('app-drawer').addEventListener('open',
    function() {...});
</script>
```

Creating and using a Shadow Root

This part describes the syntax for creating shadow DOM with the new cross-browser version (v1) of the shadow DOM specification. Shadow DOM is a new DOM feature that helps you build components. You can think of shadow DOM as a scoped subtree inside your element.

A shadow root is a document fragment that gets attached to a "host" element. The act of attaching a shadow root is how the element gains its shadow DOM. To create shadow DOM for an element call

element.attachShadow():

```
const header = document.createElement('header');
const shadowRoot = header.attachShadow({mode: 'open'});
shadowRoot.innerHTML = '<h1>Hello Shadow DOM</h1>'; // Could also
    use appendChild().
// header.shadowRoot === shadowRoot
// shadowRoot.host === header
```

Libraries for Building Web Components

Many libraries already exist that make it easier to build web components. The libraries section of the site has additional details but here are some you can try out:

- Hybrids is a UI library for creating Web Components with simple and functional API.

- Polymer provides a set of features for creating custom elements.

- LitElement uses lit-html to render into the element's Shadow DOM and adds API to help manage element properties and attributes.

- Slim.js is an opensource lightweight web component library that provides data-binding and extended capabilities for components, using es6 native class inheritance.

- Stencil is an opensource compiler that generates standards-compliant web components.

WebAssembly

```
"use strict"
const ccallArrays = (func, returnType, paramTypes=[], params, {heapIn="HEAPF32"
    , heapOut="HEAPF32", returnArraySize=1}={}) => {

    const heapMap = {}
    heapMap.HEAP8 = Int8Array    // int8_t
    heapMap.HEAPU8 = Uint8Array   // uint8_t
    heapMap.HEAP16 = Int16Array   // int16_t
    heapMap.HEAPU16 = Uint16Array  // uint16_t
    heapMap.HEAP32 = Int32Array   // int32_t
    heapMap.HEAPU32 = Uint32Array  // uint32_t
    heapMap.HEAPF32 = Float32Array // float
    heapMap.HEAPF64 = Float64Array // double

    let res
    let error
    const returnTypeParam = returnType=="array" ? "number" : returnType
    const parameters = []
    const parameterTypes = []
    const bufs = []

    try {
        if (params) {
            for (let n=0; n<params.length; n++) {
```

WebAssembly (abbreviated Wasm) is a binary instruction format for a stack-based virtual machine. Wasm is designed as a portable target for compilation of high-level languages like C/C++/Rust, enabling deployment on the web for client and server applications.

WebAssembly Features

WebAssembly is still in the early stages. The WebAssembly toolchain and implementation remain closer to proof-of-concept than production technology. That said, WebAssembly's custodians have their sights set on making WebAssembly more useful through a series of initiatives:

Garbage Collection Primitives

WebAssembly doesn't directly support languages that use garbage-collected memory models. Languages like Lua or Python can be supported only by restricting feature sets or by embedding the entire runtime as a WebAssembly executable. But there is work under way to support garbage-collected memory models regardless of the language or implementation.

Threading

Native support for threading is common to languages such as Rust and C++. The absence of threading support in WebAssembly means that whole classes of WebAssembly-targeted software can't be written in those languages. The proposal to add threading to WebAssembly uses the C++ threading model as one of its inspirations.

Bulk Memory Operations and SIMD

Bulk memory operations and SIMD (single instruction, multiple data) parallelism are must-haves for applications that grind through piles of data and need native CPU acceleration to keep from choking, like machine learning or scientific apps. Proposals are on the table to add these capabilities to WebAssembly via new operators.

High-level Language Constructs

Many other features being considered for WebAssembly map directly to high-level constructs in other languages.

- Exceptions can be emulated in WebAssembly, but cannot be implemented natively via WebAssembly's instruction set. The proposed plan for exceptions involves exception primitives compatible with the C++ exception model, which could in turn be used by other languages compiled to WebAssembly.

- Reference types make it easier to pass around objects used as references to the host environment. This would make garbage collection and a number of other high-level functions easier to implement in WebAssembly.

- Tail calls, a design pattern used in many languages.

- Functions that return multiple values, e.g., via tuples in Python or C#.

- Sign-extension operators, a useful low-level math operation. (LLVM supports these as well.)

Debugging and Profiling Tools

One of the biggest problems with transpiled JavaScript was the difficulty of debugging and profiling, due to the inability to correlate between the transpiled code and the source. With WebAssembly, we have a similar issue, and it's being addressed in a similar way (source map support).

Working of WebAssembly

WebAssembly, developed by the W3C, is in the words of its creators a "compilation target." Developers don't write WebAssembly directly; they write in the language of their choice, which is then compiled into WebAssembly bytecode. The bytecode is then run on the client—typically in a web browser—where it's translated into native machine code and executed at high speed.

WebAssembly code is meant to be faster to load, parse, and execute than JavaScript. When WebAssembly is used by a web browser, there is still the overhead of download-ing the WASM module and setting it up, but all other things being equal WebAssembly runs faster. WebAssembly also provides a sandboxed execution model, based on the same security models that exist for JavaScript now.

Right now, running WebAssembly in web browsers is the most common use case, but WebAssembly is intended to be more than a web-based solution. Eventually, as the We-bAssembly spec shapes up and more features land in it, it may become useful in mobile apps, desktop apps, servers, and other execution environments.

WebAssembly use Cases

The most basic use case for WebAssembly is as a target to write in-browser software. The components that are compiled to WebAssembly can be written in any of a number of languages; the final WebAssembly payload is then delivered through JavaScript to the client.

WebAssembly has been designed with a number of performance-intensive, brows-er-based use cases in mind: games, music streaming, video editing, CAD, encryption, and image recognition, to name just a few.

More generally, it's instructive to focus on these three areas when determining your particular WebAssembly use case:

- High-performance code that already exists in a targetable language. For in-stance, if you have a high-speed math function already written in C, and you want to incorporate it into a web application, you could deploy it as a WebAs-sembly module. The less performance-critical, user-facing parts of the app can remain in JavaScript.

- High-performance code that needs to be written from scratch, where JavaScript isn't ideal. Previously, one might have used asm.js to write such code. You can still do so, but WebAssembly is being positioned as a better long-term solution.

- Porting a desktop application to a web environment. Many of the technology demos for asm.js and WebAssembly fall into this category. WebAssembly can provide a substrate for apps that are more ambitious than just a GUI presented via HTML. This is, however, not a trivial exercise, as all the ways the desktop application interfaces with the user need to be mapped to WebAssembly/HTML/JavaScript equivalents.

If you have an existing JavaScript app that isn't pushing any performance envelopes, it's best left alone at this stage of WebAssembly's development. But if you need that app to go faster, WebAssembly may help.

WebAssembly Language Support

WebAssembly isn't meant to be written directly. As the name implies, it's more like an assembly language, something for the machine to consume, than a high-level, human-friendly programming language. WebAssembly is closer to the intermediate representation (IR) generated by the LLVM language-compiler infrastructure, than it is like C or Java.

Thus most scenarios for working with WebAssembly involve writing code in a high-level language and turning that into WebAssembly. This can be done in any of three basic ways:

- Direct compilation. The source is translated into WebAssembly by way of the language's own compiler toolchain. Rust, C/C++, Kotlin/Native, and D now all have native ways to emit WASM from compilers that support those languages.

- Third-party tools. The language doesn't have native WASM support in its toolchain, but a third-part utility can be used to convert to WASM. Java, Lua, and the .Net language family all have some support like this.

- WebAssembly-based interpreter. Here, the language itself isn't translated into WebAssembly; rather, an interpreter for the language, written in WebAssembly, runs code written in the language. This is the most cumbersome approach, since the interpreter may be several megabytes of code, but it allows existing code written in the language to run all but unchanged. Python and Ruby both have interpreters translated to WASM.

5

Web Architecture

The web architecture is a software framework which is designed with the aim of supporting the development of applications for the web, such as web resources, web services and web APIs. The topics addressed in this chapter on web browser, HTML, URL, HTTP, etc. will provide an extensive understanding of web architecture.

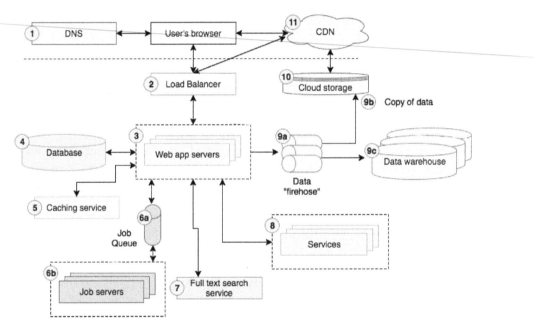

Website architecture is the planning and design of the technical, functional and visual components of a website - before it is designed, developed and deployed. It is used by website designers and developers as a means to design and develop a website.

Website architecture is used in creating a logical layout of a website in line with the user and/or business requirements. It defines the different components that will make up a website and the services each component or the website will provide in whole.

Some of the factors that are part of website architecture are:

- Technical constraints such as server, storage. memory and communication interfaces.

- Functional aspects such as the type of services or processes the website will provide.

- Visual appearance, i.e. the user interface, colors, buttons and other visual design elements.

- Security parameters i.e. how the website will ensure secure access control and transactions.

Web Application Architecture

Web application architecture defines the interactions between applications, middleware systems and databases to ensure multiple applications can work together. When a user types in a URL and taps "Go," the browser will find the Internet-facing computer the website lives on and requests that particular page.

The server then responds by sending files over to the browser. After that action, the browser executes those files to show the requested page to the user. Now, the user gets to interact with the website. Of course, all of these actions are executed within a matter of seconds. Otherwise, users wouldn't bother with websites.

What's important here is the code, which has been parsed by the browser. This very code may or may not have specific instructions telling the browser how to react to a wide swath of inputs. As a result, web application architecture includes all sub-components and external applications interchanges for an entire software application.

Of course, it is designed to function efficiently while meeting its specific needs and goals. Web application architecture is critical since the majority of global network traffic, and every single app and device uses web-based communication. It deals with scale, efficiency, robustness, and security.

Types of Web Application Architecture

Server-side HTML Web Application

Server-side HTML

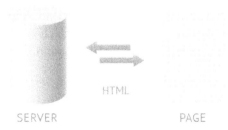

SERVER   PAGE

The most widespread web application architecture. The server generates HTML content and sends it to the client as a full-fledged HTML-page. Sometimes this architecture is called "Web 1.0", since it was the first to appear and currently dominates the sphere of web development.

Responsiveness/Usability: 1/5. The least optimal value among these architecture examples. A huge amount of data is transferred between the server and the client. The user has to wait until the whole page reloads, responding to trivial actions, for example, when only a part of the page needs to be reloaded. UI templates on the client depend directly on the frameworks applied on the server. Due to the limitations of mobile internet and huge amounts of transferred data, this architecture is hardly applicable in the mobile segment. There are no means of sending instant data updates or changes in real time. If we consider the possibility of real-time updates via generation of ready chunks of content on the server side and updates of the client (through AJAX, WebSockets), plus design with partial changes within a page, we'll go beyond this architecture.

Linkability: 5/5. The highest of the three, since it's the easiest implementable. It's due to the fact that by default one URL receives particular HTML-content on the server.

SEO: 5/5. Rather easily implemented, similarly to the previous criterion. The content is known beforehand.

Speed of development: 5/5. This is the oldest architecture in web development, so it's possible to choose any server language and framework for particular needs.

Scalability: 4/5. If we take a look at the generation of HTML, under the increasing load comes the moment when load balance will be needed. There's a much more complicated situation with scaling databases, but this task is the same for these three examples of software architecture.

Performance: 3/5. Tightly bound to responsiveness and scalability. Performance is relatively low because a big amount of data must be transferred, containing HTML, design, and business data. Therefore it's necessary to generate data for the whole page (not only for the changed business data), and all the accompanying information (such as design).

Testability: 4/5. The good thing is that there's no need for special tools, which support JavaScript interpretation, to test the front-end, and the content is static.

Security: 4/5. The application behavior logic is on the server side. However, data are transferred overtly, so a protected channel may be needed (which is basically a story of any architecture that concerns the server). All the security functionality is on the server side.

Conversion: website – mobile or desktop application: 0/5. In most cases it's simply impossible. Rarely there's an exception (more of exotics): for example, if the server is realized upon node.js, and there are no large databases; or if one utilizes third-party web services for data acquisition (however, it's a more sophisticated variant of architecture). Thus one can wrap the application in node-webkit or analogous means.

Offline work: 2/5. Implemented with a manifest on the server, which is entered to HTML5 specifications. If the browser supports such a specification, all pages of the application will be cached: in case the connection is off, the user will see a cached page.

JS Generation Widgets (AJAX)

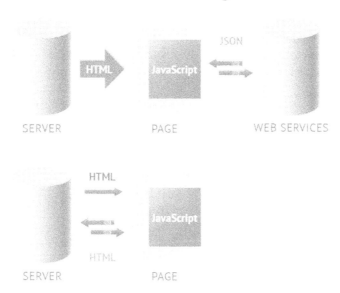

JS Generation Widgets

This is an evolved architecture of the first type. The difference is that the page, which is displayed in the browser, consists of widgets (functionally independent units). Data is uploaded to these widgets through AJAX query from the server: either as a full-fledged chunk of HTML, or as JSON, and transforms (through JavaScript templating/binding) into the content of the page. The option of uploading chunks of HTML excludes the necessity of using JavaScript-MV* frameworks on the client side; in this case something simpler can be used (for example, jQuery). By lowering interactivity we boost the development speed and make functionality cheaper and more reliable.

The foremost advantage is that updates from the server arrive only for the part of the page requested by the client. It's also good that widgets are separated functionally. A particular widget is in charge of a part of the page; partial changes will not affect the whole page.

Responsiveness/Usability: 3/5. The volume of transferred data for a part of a page is smaller than for the whole page, that's why responsiveness is higher. But since a page is a set of widgets, the applicable UI templates in a web application are limited by the chosen UI framework. Cold start (the first full loading) of such a page will take a little longer. The content, which is fully generated and cached on the server, can be instantly displayed on the client; here time is spent on getting the data for the widget and, as a rule, on templating. At the first visit the website will not be that quick to load, but further it will be much more pleasant in use, if compared to sites based on the architecture of the first type. Also it's worth to mention the possibility of implementation of "partial" loading (like it's done on yahoo.com).

Linkability: 2/5. Here special tools and mechanisms are needed. As a rule, Hash-Bang mechanism is applied.

SEO: 2/5. There are special mechanisms for these tasks. For example, for promotion of websites based on this architecture it's possible to predefine the list of promoted pages and make static URLs for them, without parameters and modifiers.

Speed of development: 3/5. One needs to know the server-side technologies in web development, and use JavaScript frameworks on the client side. It's also required to implement web services on the server side.

Performance: 4/5. The time and resources spent on generation of HTML content are relatively minor if compared to the time spent by the app on retrieving data from the databases, and on their processing before templating. Use of the extended type of this architecture (when data are transferred as JSON) lowers the traffic between the client and the server, but adds an abstraction level to the application: retrieval from database -> data processing, serialization in JSON -> API: JSON -> parsing of JSON -> binding of data object on the client to HTML.

Scalability: 4/5. Same as for the first type of architecture.

Testability: 1/5. It's required to test the server side, the client code, and the web service which returns the data to update widgets.

Security: 4/5. Part of the logic is shifted to the client JavaScript which can be modified by an intruder.

Conversion: website – mobile or desktop application: 0/5. Same as for the first type of architecture.

Offline work: 1/5. The manifest mechanism works in this case, but there's a problem with updating or caching the data displayed on the widget. This functionality has to be implemented additionally: in the manifest one can indicate only names of the files that will be cached from the server. Correlation between the widget template file, cached in the manifest, and the page behavior logic requires extra effort.

Service-oriented Single-page Web Apps (Web 2.0, HTML5 apps)

The term "Web 2.0" isn't quite correct here. One of peculiarities of Web 2.0 is the principle of involving users into filling and repeated adjustments of content. Basically the term "Web 2.0" means projects and services which are actively developed and improved by users themselves: blogs, wikis, social networks. This means Web 2.0 isn't bound to one technology or a set of technologies.

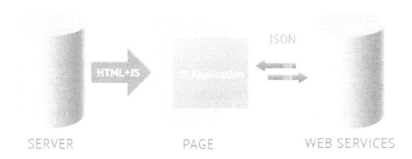

Let's figure out the essence of this architecture. An HTML-page is downloaded from the server. This page is a container for JavaScript code, which addresses a particular web service and retrieves business data only. The data is used by JavaScript application, which generates the HTML content of the page. This architecture is a self-sufficient and rather complex JavaScript application, where part of the functionality is shifted to the client side. To compare, the architecture of the second type cannot show a high number of interrelated and structured functions.

In modern web development, fully offline JavaScript apps are rare (with a few exceptions, e.g. rad-js.com). This approach allows an easily made reverse conversion: publish an existing application on the web.

Responsiveness/Usability: 5/5. The volume of data transferred for updates, is minimal. That's why responsiveness is at the highest level. UI is generated via JavaScript, it's possible to implement any necessary variants. There is an issue with multithreading in JavaScript: in this particular case processing of big volumes of business data should be shifted to the web service.

Linkability: 1/5. One will need special tools and mechanisms, as well as frameworks which can use, for example, Hash-Bang mechanism.

SEO: 1/5. The hardest one to promote. If the entire app is promoted directly, there's no problem: it's possible to promote the application container. If it's needed for a part of the application, a special mechanism will be needed for that purpose. Each more or less big search engine offers its own methods of standartization for this process.

Speed of development: 2/5. It's required to develop a web service and apply more specialized JavaScript frameworks which build the app architecture. Since the architecture is relatively new, there aren't many specialists who are able to create a high-quality site/system based on this approach. There aren't many time-tested tools, frameworks and approaches.

Performance: 5/5. This criterion is the least influenced on by the server side. The server only has to give the JavaScript application to the browser. On the client side, performance and browser type are of the biggest importance.

Scalability: 5/5. The web logic is on the client side. There is no content generation on the server. When there's an increase in the number of users, it's required to scale only the web services that give the business data.

Testability: 3/5. It's required to test web services and the client JavaScript code.

Security: 0/5. The logic is shifted to the client JavaScript, which can be relatively easily modified by an intruder. For protected systems it's required to develop a preventive architecture, which considers the peculiarities of open-source applications.

Conversion: website – mobile or desktop application: 5/5. A website becomes an application with the help of PhoneGap or a similar platform.

Offline work: 5/5. This architecture is a full-fledged application; it's possible to save separate data, as well as parts of the application using any storage (for example, local storage). One more advantage is the possibility to switch data storage and management to the offline mode. To compare, the two aforementioned architectures are only partially functional in the offline mode. Here the missing data can be replaced with mocks, it's possible to show alert windows or use data from the local storage, while synchronization may be left for later.

Working of Web Application Architecture

With web applications, you have the server vs. the client side. In essence, there are two programs running concurrently:

- The code which lives in the browser and responds to user input
- The code which lives on the server and responds to HTTP request

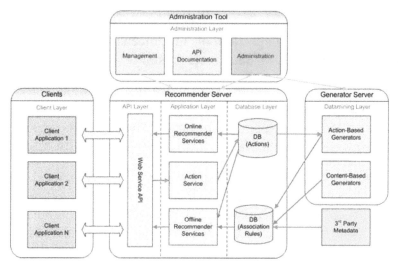

When writing an app, it is up to the web developer to decide what the code on the server should do in relation to what the code on the browser should do. With server-side code, languages include:

- Ruby on Rails

- PHP

- C#

- Java

- Python

- Javascript

In fact, any code that can respond to HTTP requests has the capability to run on a server. Here are a few other attributes of server-side code:

- Is never seen by the user (except within a rare malfunction)

- Stores data such as user profiles, tweets, pages, etc.

- Creates the page the user requested

With client-side code, languages used include:

- CSS

- Javascript

- HTML

These are then parsed by the user's browser. Moreover, client-side code can be seen and edited by the user. Plus, it has to communicate only through HTTP requests and cannot read files off of a server directly. Furthermore, it reacts to user input.

The reason why it is imperative to have good web application architecture is because it is the blueprint for supporting future growth which may come from increased demand, future interoperability and enhanced reliability requirements. Through object-oriented programming, the organizational design of web application architecture defines precisely how an application will function. Some features include:

- Delivering persistent data through HTTP, which can be understood by client-side code and vice-versa

- Making sure requests contain valid data

- Offers authentication for users

- Limits what users can see based on permissions

- Creates, updates and deletes records

Trends in Web Application Architecture

As technology continues to evolve, so does web application architecture. One such trend is the use of and creation of service-oriented architecture. This is where most of the code for the entire application exists as services. In addition, each has its own HTTP API. As a result, one facet of the code can make a request to another part of the code—which may be running on a different server.

Another trend is a single-page application. This is where web UI is presented through a rich JavaScript application. It then stays in the user's browser over a variety of interactions. In terms of requests, it uses AJAX or WebSockets for performing asynchronous or synchronous requests to the web server without having to load the page.

The user then gets a more natural experience with limited page load interruptions. At their core, many web applications are built around objects. The objects are stored in tables via an SQL database. Each row in a table has a particular record. So, with relational databases, it is all about relations. You can call on records just by listing the row and column for a target data point.

With the two above trends, web apps are now much better suited for viewing on multiple platforms and multiple devices. Even when most of the code for the apps remain the same, they can still be viewed clearly and easily on a smaller screen.

Best Practices for Good Web Application Architecture

You may have a working app, but it also needs to have good web architecture. Here are several attributes necessary for good web application architecture:

- Solves problems consistently and uniformly
- Is as simple as possible
- Supports the latest standards include A/B testing and analytics
- Offers fast response times
- Utilizes security standards to reduce the chance of malicious penetrations
- Does not crash
- Heals itself
- Does not have a single point of failure
- Scales out easily
- Allows for easy creation of known data
- Errors logged in a user-friendly way
- Automated deployments

The reason the above factors are necessary is because, with the right attributes, you can build a better app. Not to mention, by supporting horizontal and vertical growth, software deployment is much more efficient, user-friendly and reliable.

Architectural Designs used for Web Applications

Client-side Static Mashup

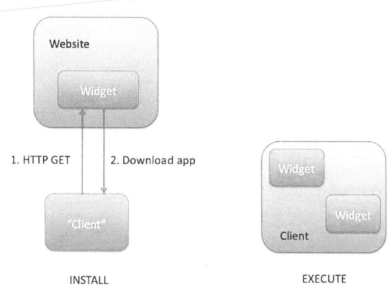

INSTALL   EXECUTE

The client downloads an application that then runs locally. These applications are often called "widgets". Typically, the client sends some data to the website, perhaps by filling a form, and a customized widget is downloaded.

The data submitted by the user may be sensetive so security and privacy considerations apply.

Trust

Trust between the client and the widget source is established by using crypto signatures. Trust is often proxied by use of an "app-store" model.

Marcos Cacares disagrees. He says: The Digital Signature spec says "Widget authors and distributors can digitally sign widgets as a mechanism to ensure continuity of authorship and distributorship. Prior to instantiation, a user agent can use the digital signature to verify the integrity of the widget package and to confirm the signing key(s)." However, this should not be confused with "trust" in any way (e.g., an author I trust could turn evil, or the widget could be hijacked).

Re. app-store he says: an appstore cannot really guarantee trust (as above). There are lots of trust models that will hopefully emerge around widgets (such as community mediated trust - where a community needs to approve something as safe before it can be used on devices). Depending on single points of trust is a bad thing, IMO. The central idea is that anyone can be an app store and that (hopefully) widgets engines will be able to get widgets from anywhere on the Web (i.e., totally decentralized distribution model).

There is also the question of whether the form should be trusted. If the form came from the same authority as the URI assignment authority, then it is definitely trustworthy but if it comes from some other authority then it might be trustworthy.

Client-side URIs

When the widget starts it displays a URI. As the application proceeds, for example, by scrolling on a map, the URI changes. These URIs are constructed dynamically but conform to general URI usage, i.e. they can be stored on the server, sent to others in email, etc.

Server-side Static Mashup

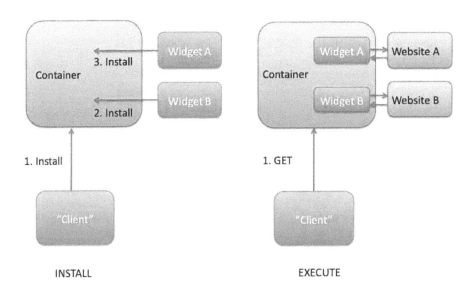

- Widgets on the server-side

- No separate download step, but often requires installation of content to a "container"

- One website combines content from multiple other websites, often by means of iFrames

- External content validated statically by (for example) Caja, FBJS

- DNS-based trust, proxied by "container" site

Client-side Dynamic Mashup

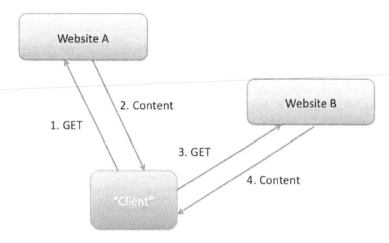

- One site creates content which includes requests for content to other sites, or for information provided by the client

- Content is assembled dynamically on the client, based on content from multiple places

- Trust based on a combination of "user grant", enforcement of restrictions such as SOP, and other techniques (CORS, UMP, OAuth et al)

General Web Application Architecture

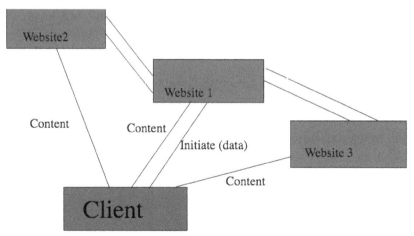

The general architecture for Web Applications can be described as a user, from a browser, initiating an application that may run on one or more websites. The websites communicate to one another and may exchange data or start processes.

The user initiates the application on one websites, sending parameters and other customizing information to it. This website may enlist the aid of other websites. The display on the user's browser, in general, may consist of data from several websites.

In some cases, code may be transferred to run on the user's browser.

In addition to the usual concerns with browsers and URIs this architecture provides several additional challenges. For example:

- Secure communication between the websites

- Trust between the cooperating websites

- Need for client-side storage

Client-side Storage

Note that the multiple websites in this model could be copies of the same website. Thus, you could be executing a single transaction in which you buy two different airline tickets from the same website. If you use cookies to remember the details of the tickets, the cookies would go to both copies of the website and the details of the tickets would get mixed up.

What is needed is, clearly, separate "cookies" for each copy of the website. The Web Applications WG is attempting to address this requirement with a facility called session storage. This essentially, provides a local database that can be used to store name-value pairs for each session with a website.

The second requirement comes from a situation where the user is working with multiple windows, and wants the session to persist across interruptions in connectivity. To enable this a local database can be used to store name-value pairs and this data can be used while the website is offline.

Again, cookies do not handle this case well, because they are transmitted with every request. This requirement is also being addressed by the Web Applications WG with a facility called Local Storage which allows name-value pairs to be stored locally. Such a facility can also be used to improve performance. The user may wish to store megabytes of user data, such as entire user-authored documents or a user's mailbox, on the client side and work on them offline.

While session storage and local storage provide simple name-value pair storage to cover the abovementioned usecases, they do not provide advanced "database" facilities such as in-order retrieval of keys, efficient searching over values, r storage of duplicate values for a key. To provide such facilities the Web Applications WG is working on a specification called Indexed Database API. A competing specification that provides similar capabilities called Web SQL Database. This specification seems to be on hold for the time being. Some have argued against it because, despite its name, it does not follow the SQL standard. Others have argued against it because it is based on a proprietary product and it is difficult to get two independent implementations.

Web Browser

A web browser is application software that is used to present or receive resources that is traversing through the World Wide Web (www). An information resource can be images, videos, web pages or any other content identified by URL. Browsers plays the client side interface role in Client Server Architecture. Browser allow client device to connect to a webserver and read the HTML files located on it. When the web browser send request to web server, these files are transferred to your computer as response that is interpreted by web browser to display the content. In the easiest words we can describe a web browser as a tool or software to surf internet quickly and efficiently. Some of the most common and popular web browsers can be named as Microsoft Edge (Internet Explorer), Google Chrome, Apple Safari, Mozilla Firefox, Netscape, Opera etc.

Web browsers, now-a-days, are well functioned software packages that can easily translate and display applications, html page, JavaScript, Ajax etc. related contents on web server. Web browsers also offer plugins for better performance and multimedia contents. Although web browsers are mainly used to work with World Wide Web, it can also be utilized for accessing information & resources provided by web server in private networks.

Function of Web Browser

The main functions of web browser is to fctch or retrieve informative resources from World Wide Web to the client/ user on demand, translate those files received from web server and display those content to the user and allow the client /user to access all other relevant resources & information via hyperlinks.

When the user inputs any URL (uniform resource locator) in the web browser, the user is navigated to that website by the browser quickly. Let us have a look on its processing. When user type any URL, for example https://msatechnosoft.in, the prefix of the URL decide how to retrieve it. The URL prefixes that the web browser is not able to handle directly is sent to related application. Like default email app is responsible to handle mailto: URL prefix. Following table gives an idea about some of the common URL prefixes:

URL Prefix	URL Interpretation
http:	Hypertext transfer protocol
https:	Secured hypertext transfer protocol
ftp:	File transfer protocol
file:	Local file system

Plugins are available on web browser that supports flash content and java applets to run smoothly in any device.

Web browser allow users to interact with web pages and other dynamic contents via hyperlinks that provides navigation facility i.e. to go to different locations by clicking on links that makes internet surfing easy.

Web browsers are software installed on your PC. To access the Web, you need a web browser, such as Netscape Navigator, Microsoft Internet Explorer or Mozilla Firefox.

Currently you must be using any sort of Web browser while you are navigating through a site. On the Web, when you navigate through pages of information, this is commonly known as web browsing or web surfing.

There are four leading web browsers – Explorer, Firefox, Netscape, and Safari, but there are many others browsers available. You might be interested in knowing Complete Browser Statistics. Now we will see these browsers in bit more detail.

While developing a site, we should try to make it compatible to as many browsers as possible. Especially sites should be compatible to major browsers like Explorer, Firefox, Chrome, Netscape, Opera, and Safari.

 ## Internet Explorer

Internet Explorer (IE) is a product from software giant Microsoft. This is the most commonly used browser in the universe. This was introduced in 1995 along with Windows 95 launch and it has passed Netscape popularity in 1998.

 ## Google Chrome

This web browser is developed by Google and its beta version was first released on September 2, 2008 for Microsoft Windows. Today, chrome is known to be one of the most popular web browsers with its global share of more than 50%.

Mozilla Firefox

Firefox is a new browser derived from Mozilla. It was released in 2004 and has grown to be the second most popular browser on the Internet.

 ## Safari

Safari is a web browser developed by Apple Inc. and included in Mac OS X. It was first released as a public beta in January 2003. Safari has very good support for latest technologies like XHTML, CSS2 etc.

 ## Opera

Opera is smaller and faster than most other browsers, yet it is full- featured. Fast, user-friendly, with keyboard interface, multiple windows, zoom functions, and more. Java and non Java-enabled versions available. Ideal for newcomers to the Internet, school children, handicap and as a front-end for CD-Rom and kiosks.

 ## Konqueror

Konqueror is an Open Source web browser with HTML 4.01 compliance, supporting Java applets, JavaScript, CSS 1, CSS 2.1, as well as Netscape plugins. This works as a file manager as well as it supports basic file management on local UNIX filesystems, from simple cut/copy and paste operations to advanced remote and local network file browsing.

 ## Lynx

Lynx is a fully-featured World Wide Web browser for users on Unix, VMS, and other platforms running cursor-addressable, character-cell terminals or emulators.

HTML

HTML is the standard markup language for creating Web pages.

- HTML stands for Hyper Text Markup Language
- HTML describes the structure of Web pages using markup
- HTML elements are the building blocks of HTML pages
- HTML elements are represented by tags

- HTML tags label pieces of content such as "heading", "paragraph", "table", and so on

- Browsers do not display the HTML tags, but use them to render the content of the page

A Simple HTML Document

Example

```
<!DOCTYPE html>
    <html>
    <head>
    <title>Page Title</title>
    </head>
    <body>

    <h1>My First Heading</h1>
    <p>My first paragraph.</p>

    </body>
    </html>
```

Example Explained

- The <!DOCTYPE html> declaration defines this document to be HTML5
- The <html> element is the root element of an HTML page
- The <head> element contains meta information about the document
- The <title> element specifies a title for the document
- The <body> element contains the visible page content
- The <h1> element defines a large heading
- The <p> element defines a paragraph

HTML Tags

HTML tags are element names surrounded by angle brackets:

<tagname>content goes here...</tagname>

- HTML tags normally come in pairs like <p> and </p>

- The first tag in a pair is the start tag, the second tag is the end tag

- The end tag is written like the start tag, but with a forward slash inserted before the tag name

Web Browsers

The purpose of a web browser (Chrome, IE, Firefox, Safari) is to read HTML documents and display them.

The browser does not display the HTML tags, but uses them to determine how to display the document:

HTML Page Structure

Below is a visualization of an HTML page structure:

```
<html>
<head>
<title>Page title</title>
</head>
<body>
<h1>This is a heading</h1>
<p>This is a paragraph.</p>
<p>This is another paragraph.</p>
</body>
</html>
```

<!DOCTYPE> Declaration

The <!DOCTYPE> declaration represents the document type, and helps browsers to display web pages correctly.

It must only appear once, at the top of the page (before any HTML tags).

The <!DOCTYPE> declaration is not case sensitive.

The <!DOCTYPE> declaration for HTML5 is:

HTML Versions

Since the early days of the web, there have been many versions of HTML:

Version	Year
HTML	1991
HTML 2.0	1995
HTML 3.2	1997
HTML 4.01	1999
XHTML	2000
HTML5	2014

HTML Documents

All HTML documents must start with a document type declaration: <!DOCTYPE html>.

The HTML document itself begins with <html> and ends with </html>.

The visible part of the HTML document is between <body> and </body>.

Example

```
<!DOCTYPE html>
    <html>
    <body>

    <h1>My First Heading</h1>
    <p>My first paragraph.</p>

    </body>
    </html>
```

HTML Headings

HTML headings are defined with the <h1> to <h6> tags.

<h1> defines the most important heading. <h6> defines the least important heading:

Example

> <h1>This is heading 1</h1>
>
> <h2>This is heading 2</h2>
>
> <h3>This is heading 3</h3>

HTML Paragraphs

> HTML paragraphs are defined with the <p> tag:

Example

> <p>This is a paragraph.</p>
>
> <p>This is another paragraph.</p>

HTML Links

> HTML links are defined with the <a> tag:

Example

> <a href="https://www.w3schools.com">This is a link</a>

The link's destination is specified in the href attribute.

Attributes are used to provide additional information about HTML elements.

HTML Images

HTML images are defined with the <img> tag.

The source file (src), alternative text (alt), width, and height are provided as attributes:

Example

> <img src="w3schools.jpg" alt="W3Schools.com" width="104" height="142">

HTML Buttons

> HTML buttons are defined with the <button> tag:

Example

```
<button>Click me</button>
```

HTML Lists

HTML lists are defined with the <ul> (unordered/bullet list) or the <ol> (ordered/numbered list) tag, followed by <li> tags (list items):

Example

```
<ul>
  <li>Coffee</li>
  <li>Tea</li>
  <li>Milk</li>
</ul>
```

HTML Elements

An HTML element usually consists of a start tag and end tag, with the content inserted in between:

```
<tagname>Content goes here...</tagname>
```

The HTML element is everything from the start tag to the end tag:

```
<p>My first paragraph.</p>
```

Start tag	Element content	End tag
<h1>	My First Heading	</h1>
<p>	My first paragraph.	</p>

Nested HTML Elements

HTML elements can be nested (elements can contain elements).

All HTML documents consist of nested HTML elements.

This example contains four HTML elements:

Example

```
<!DOCTYPE html>
  <html>
  <body>
```

```
<h1>My First Heading</h1>
<p>My first paragraph.</p>

</body>
</html>
```

Example Explained

The <html> element defines the whole document.

It has a start tag <html> and an end tag </html>.

The element content is another HTML element (the <body> element).

```
<html>
    <body>

    <h1>My First Heading</h1>
    <p>My first paragraph.</p>

    </body>
</html>
```

The <body> element defines the document body.

It has a start tag <body> and an end tag </body>.

The element content is two other HTML elements (<h1> and <p>).

```
<body>

    <h1>My First Heading</h1>
    <p>My first paragraph.</p>

    </body>
```

The <h1> element defines a heading.

It has a start tag <h1> and an end tag </h1>.

The element content is: My First Heading.

```
<h1>My First Heading</h1>
```

The <p> element defines a paragraph.

```
It has a start tag <p> and an end tag </p>.
```

The element content is: My first paragraph.

```
<p>My first paragraph.</p>
```

Example

```
<html>
    <body>

    <p>This is a paragraph
    <p>This is a paragraph

    </body>
    </html>
```

The example above works in all browsers, because the closing tag is considered option-al.

Never rely on this. It might produce unexpected results and/or errors if you forget the end tag.

Empty HTML Elements

HTML elements with no content are called empty elements.

 is an empty element without a closing tag (the <br> tag defines a line break).

Empty elements can be "closed" in the opening tag like this: <br />.

HTML5 does not require empty elements to be closed. But if you want stricter valida-tion, or if you need to make your document readable by XML parsers, you must close all HTML elements properly.

Use Lowercase Tags

HTML tags are not case sensitive: <P> means the same as <p>.

The HTML5 standard does not require lowercase tags, but W3C recommends lower-case in HTML, and demands lowercase for stricter document types like XHTML.

HTML Attributes

Attributes provide additional information about HTML elements.

HTML Attributes

- All HTML elements can have attributes
- Attributes provide additional information about an element
- Attributes are always specified in the start tag
- Attributes usually come in name/value pairs like: name="value"

Href Attribute

HTML links are defined with the <a> tag. The link address is specified in the href attribute:

Example

```
<a href="https://www.w3schools.com">This is a link</a>
```

Src Attribute

HTML images are defined with the <img> tag.

The filename of the image source is specified in the src attribute:

Example

```
<img src="img_girl.jpg">
```

The Width and Height Attributes

Images in HTML have a set of size attributes, which specifies the width and height of the image:

Example

```
<img src="img_girl.jpg" width="500" height="600">
```

The image size is specified in pixels: width="500" means 500 pixels wide.

Alt Attribute

The alt attribute specifies an alternative text to be used, when an image cannot be displayed.

The value of the attribute can be read by screen readers. This way, someone "listening" to the webpage, e.g. a blind person, can "hear" the element.

Example

```
<img src="img_girl.jpg" alt="Girl with a jacket">
```

Example

See what happens if we try to display an image that does not exist:

```
<img src="img_typo.jpg" alt="Girl with a jacket">
```

Style Attribute

The style attribute is used to specify the styling of an element, like color, font, size etc.

Example

```
<p style="color:red">I am a paragraph</p>
```

Lang Attribute

The language of the document can be declared in the <html> tag.

The language is declared with the lang attribute.

Declaring a language is important for accessibility applications (screen readers) and search engines:

```
<!DOCTYPE html>
    <html lang="en-US">
    <body>

    . . .

    </body>
    </html>
```

The first two letters specify the language (en). If there is a dialect, use two more letters (US).

Title Attribute

Here, a title attribute is added to the <p> element. The value of the title attribute will be displayed as a tooltip when you mouse over the paragraph:

We Suggest: Use Lowercase Attributes

The HTML5 standard does not require lowercase attribute names.

The title attribute can be written with uppercase or lowercase like title or TITLE.

W3C recommends lowercase in HTML, and demands lowercase for stricter document types like XHTML.

We Suggest: Quote Attribute Values

The HTML5 standard does not require quotes around attribute values.

The href attribute, demonstrated above, can be written without quotes:

Single or Double Quotes

Double quotes around attribute values are the most common in HTML, but single quotes can also be used.

In some situations, when the attribute value itself contains double quotes, it is necessary to use single quotes:

HTML Links

Links are found in nearly all web pages. Links allow users to click their way from page to page.

HTML Links - Hyperlinks

HTML links are hyperlinks.

You can click on a link and jump to another document.

When you move the mouse over a link, the mouse arrow will turn into a little hand.

HTML Links - Syntax

In HTML, links are defined with the <a> tag:

```
<a href="url">link text</a>
```

The href attribute specifies the destination address of the link.

Clicking on the link text will send you to the specified address.

Local Links

The example above used an absolute URL (a full web address).

A local link (link to the same web site) is specified with a relative URL

HTML Links - Create a Bookmark

HTML bookmarks are used to allow readers to jump to specific parts of a Web page.

Bookmarks can be useful if your webpage is very long.

To make a bookmark, you must first create the bookmark, and then add a link to it.

When the link is clicked, the page will scroll to the location with the bookmark.

Example

First, create a bookmark with the id attribute:

External Paths

External pages can be referenced with a full URL or with a path relative to the current web page.

This example uses a full URL to link to a web page:

A URL is another word for a web address.

A URL can be composed of words, or an Internet Protocol (IP) address (192.68.20.50).

Most people enter the name when surfing, because names are easier to remember than numbers.

URL - Uniform Resource Locator

Web browsers request pages from web servers by using a URL.

A Uniform Resource Locator (URL) is used to address a document (or other data) on the web.

Explanation:

- scheme - defines the type of Internet service (most common is http or https)
- prefix - defines a domain prefix (default for http is www)
- domain - defines the Internet domain name (like w3schools.com)
- port - defines the port number at the host (default for http is 80)
- path - defines a path at the server (If omitted: the root directory of the site)
- filename - defines the name of a document or resource

Common URL Schemes

The table below lists some common schemes:

Scheme	Short for	Used for
http	HyperText Transfer Protocol	Common web pages. Not encrypted
https	Secure HyperText Transfer Protocol	Secure web pages. Encrypted
ftp	File Transfer Protocol	Downloading or uploading files
file		A file on your computer

URL Encoding

URLs can only be sent over the Internet using the ASCII character-set. If a URL contains characters outside the ASCII set, the URL has to be converted.

URL encoding converts non-ASCII characters into a format that can be transmitted over the Internet.

URL encoding replaces non-ASCII characters with a "%" followed by hexadecimal digits.

URLs cannot contain spaces. URL encoding normally replaces a space with a plus (+) sign, or %20.

If you click "Submit", the browser will URL encode the input before it is sent to the server.

A page at the server will display the received input.

Try some other input and click Submit again.

ASCII Encoding Examples

Your browser will encode input, according to the character-set used in your page.

The default character-set in HTML5 is UTF-8.

Character	From Windows-1252	From UTF-8
€	%80	%E2%82%AC
£	%A3	%C2%A3
©	%A9	%C2%A9
®	%AE	%C2%AE
À	%C0	%C3%80
Á	%C1	%C3%81
Â	%C2	%C3%82
Ã	%C3	%C3%83
Ä	%C4	%C3%84
Å	%C5	%C3%85

The DOCTYPE declaration for HTML5 is very simple:

```
<!DOCTYPE html>
```

The character encoding (charset) declaration is also very simple:

```
<meta charset="UTF-8">
```

New HTML5 Elements

The most interesting new HTML5 elements are:

```
<!DOCTYPE html>
   <html>
   <head>
   <meta charset="UTF-8">
   <title>Title of the document</title>
   </head>

   <body>
   Content of the document......
   </body>

   </html>
```

New semantic elements like <header>, <footer>, <article>, and <section>.

New attributes of form elements like number, date, time, calendar, and range.

New graphic elements: <svg> and <canvas>.

New multimedia elements: <audio> and <video>.

New HTML5 API's (Application Programming Interfaces)

The most interesting new API's in HTML5 are:

- HTML Geolocation

- HTML Drag and Drop

- HTML Local Storage

- HTML Application Cache

- HTML Web Workers

- HTML SSE

Removed Elements in HTML5

The following HTML4 elements have been removed in HTML5:

Removed Element	Use Instead
<acronym>	<abbr>
<applet>	<object>
<basefont>	CSS
<big>	CSS
<center>	CSS
<dir>	<ul>
<font>	CSS
<frame>	
<frameset>	
<noframes>	
<strike>	CSS, <s>, or <del>
<tt>	CSS

Typical HTML4	Typical HTML5
<div id="header">	<header>
<div id="menu">	<nav>
<div id="content">	<section>
<div class="article">	<article>
<div id="footer">	<footer>

HTML Multimedia

Multimedia on the web is sound, music, videos, movies, and animations.

Multimedia comes in many different formats. It can be almost anything you can hear or see.

Examples: Images, music, sound, videos, records, films, animations, and more.

Web pages often contain multimedia elements of different types and formats.

Here, you will learn about the different multimedia formats.

Browser Support

The first web browsers had support for text only, limited to a single font in a single color.

Later came browsers with support for colors and fonts, and images.

Audio, video, and animation have been handled differently by the major browsers. Different formats have been supported, and some formats require extra helper programs (plug-ins) to work.

Hopefully this will become history. HTML5 multimedia promises an easier future for multimedia.

Multimedia Formats

Multimedia elements (like audio or video) are stored in media files.

The most common way to discover the type of a file, is to look at the file extension.

Multimedia files have formats and different extensions like: .swf, .wav, .mp3, .mp4, .mpg, .wmv, and .avi.

Common Video Formats

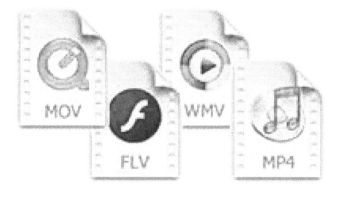

Format	File	Description
MPEG	.mpg .mpeg	MPEG. Developed by the Moving Pictures Expert Group. The first popular video format on the web. Used to be supported by all browsers, but it is not supported in HTML5 .
AVI	.avi	AVI (Audio Video Interleave). Developed by Microsoft. Commonly used in video cameras and TV hardware. Plays well on Windows computers, but not in web browsers.
WMV	.wmv	WMV (Windows Media Video). Developed by Microsoft. Commonly used in video cameras and TV hardware. Plays well on Windows computers, but not in web browsers.
QuickTime	.mov	QuickTime. Developed by Apple. Commonly used in video cameras and TV hardware. Plays well on Apple computers, but not in web browsers.
RealVideo	.rm .ram	RealVideo. Developed by Real Media to allow video streaming with low bandwidths. It is still used for online video and Internet TV, but does not play in web browsers.
Flash	.swf .flv	Flash. Developed by Macromedia. Often requires an extra component (plug-in) to play in web browsers.
Ogg	.ogg	Theora Ogg. Developed by the Xiph.Org Foundation. Supported by HTML5.
WebM	.webm	WebM. Developed by the web giants, Mozilla, Opera, Adobe, and Google. Supported by HTML5.
MPEG-4 or MP4	.mp4	MP4. Developed by the Moving Pictures Expert Group. Based on QuickTime. Commonly used in newer video cameras and TV hardware. Supported by all HTML5 browsers. Recommended by YouTube.

Audio Formats

MP3 is the newest format for compressed recorded music. The term MP3 has become synonymous with digital music.

If your website is about recorded music, MP3 is the choice.

Format	File	Description
MIDI	.mid .midi	MIDI (Musical Instrument Digital Interface). Main format for all electronic music devices like synthesizers and PC sound cards. MIDI files do not contain sound, but digital notes that can be played by electronics. Plays well on all computers and music hardware, but not in web browsers.
RealAudio	.rm .ram	RealAudio. Developed by Real Media to allow streaming of audio with low bandwidths. Does not play in web browsers.
WMA	.wma	WMA (Windows Media Audio). Developed by Microsoft. Commonly used in music players. Plays well on Windows computers, but not in web browsers.
AAC	.aac	AAC (Advanced Audio Coding). Developed by Apple as the default format for iTunes. Plays well on Apple computers, but not in web browsers.

WAV	.wav	WAV. Developed by IBM and Microsoft. Plays well on Windows, Macintosh, and Linux operating systems. Supported by HTML5.
Ogg	.ogg	Ogg. Developed by the Xiph.Org Foundation. Supported by HTML5.
MP3	.mp3	MP3 files are actually the sound part of MPEG files. MP3 is the most popular format for music players. Combines good compression (small files) with high quality. Supported by all browsers.
MP4	.mp4	MP4 is a video format, but can also be used for audio. MP4 video is the up-coming video format on the internet. This leads to automatic support for MP4 audio by all browsers.

HTML5 Video

Playing Videos in HTML

Before HTML5, a video could only be played in a browser with a plug-in (like flash).

The HTML5 <video> element specifies a standard way to embed a video in a web page.

Browser Support

The numbers in the table specify the first browser version that fully supports the <video> element.

Element	●	e	●	◉	O
<video>	4.0	9.0	3.5	4.0	10.5

HTML <video> Element

To show a video in HTML, use the <video> element:

```
Example

<video width="320" height="240" controls>
    <source src="movie.mp4" type="video/mp4">
    <source src="movie.ogg" type="video/ogg">
  Your browser does not support the video tag.
    </video>
```

Working of Control Attributes

The controls attribute adds video controls, like play, pause, and volume.

It is a good idea to always include width and height attributes. If height and width are not set, the page might flicker while the video loads.

The <source> element allows you to specify alternative video files which the browser may choose from. The browser will use the first recognized format.

The text between the <video> and </video> tags will only be displayed in browsers that do not support the <video> element.

HTML <video> Autoplay

To start a video automatically use the autoplay attribute:

```
Example

<video width="320" height="240" autoplay>
    <source src="movie.mp4" type="video/mp4">
    <source src="movie.ogg" type="video/ogg">
 Your browser does not support the video tag.
    </video>
```

HTML Video - Browser Support

In HTML5, there are 3 supported video formats: MP4, WebM, and Ogg.

The browser support for the different formats is:

Browser	MP4	WebM	Ogg
Internet Explorer	YES	NO	NO
Chrome	YES	YES	YES
Firefox	YES	YES	YES
Safari	YES	NO	NO
Opera	YES (from Opera 25)	YES	YES

HTML Video - Media Types

File Format	Media Type
MP4	video/mp4
WebM	video/webm
Ogg	video/ogg

HTML Video - Methods, Properties, and Events

HTML5 defines DOM methods, properties, and events for the <video> element.

This allows you to load, play, and pause videos, as well as setting duration and volume.

There are also DOM events that can notify you when a video begins to play, is paused, etc.

HTML Audio - Browser Support

In HTML5, there are 3 supported audio formats: MP3, WAV, and OGG.

The browser support for the different formats is:

Browser	MP3	WAV	OGG
Internet Explorer	YES	NO	NO
Chrome	YES	YES	YES
Firefox	YES	YES	YES
Safari	YES	YES	NO
Opera	YES	YES	YES

HTML Audio - Media Types

File Format	Media Type
MP3	audio/mpeg
OGG	audio/ogg
WAV	audio/wav

HTML Audio - Methods, Properties, and Events

HTML5 defines DOM methods, properties, and events for the <audio> element.

This allows you to load, play, and pause audios, as well as set duration and volume.

There are also DOM events that can notify you when an audio begins to play, is paused, etc.

URI

URI stands for Uniform Resource Identifier, and it's the official name for those things you see all the time on the Web that begin 'http:' or 'mailto:', for example http://www. w3.org/, which is the URI for the home page of the World Wide Web consortium. (These things were called URLs, for Uniform Resource Locators, in the early days of the Web, and the change from URL to URI is either hugely significant or completely irrelevant, depending on who's talking—one won't have anything to say about this issue here. If you've never heard of URIs (or IRIs, the even more recent fully internationalised version), but are familiar with URLs, just think 'URL' whenever you see 'URI' below.)

Historically, URIs were mostly seen as simply the way you accessed web pages. These pages were hand-authored, relatively stable and simply shipped out on demand. More and more often that is not the case: in at least three different ways:

Web pages for reading have been complemented by pictures for viewing, videos for watching and music for listening;

The Web is now more than a conduit for information, it's a means to a variety of ends: we use it to do things: purchase goods and services, contribute to forums, play games;

The things we access on the Web are often not hand-authored or stable, but are automatically synthesised from 'deeper' data sources on demand. Furthermore, that synthesis is increasingly influenced by aspects of the way we initiate the access.

It's against this background that I think it's worth exploring with some care what URIs were meant to be, and how they are being used in practice. In particular, I want to look at what illumination might be contributed from our understanding of how other kinds of identifiers work.

The Official Version

Insofar as there are definitive documents about all this, they all agree that URIs are, as the third initial says, identifiers, that is, names. They identify resources, and often (although not always) allow you to access representations of those resources. (Words in bold are used as technical terms—their ordinary language meaning is in many cases likely to be more confusing than helpful.)

'Resource' names a role in a story, not an intrinsically distinguishable subset of things, just as 'referent' does in ordinary language. Things are resources because someone created a URI to identify them, not because they have some particular properties in and of themselves.

'Representation' names a pair: a character sequence and a media type. The media type specifies how the character string should be interpreted. For example JPG or HTML or MP3 would be likely media types for representations of an image of an apple, a news report about an orchard or a recording of a Beatles song, respectively.

The relationship of these three concepts (URI, resource, representation) per the official version is illustrated in this diagram:

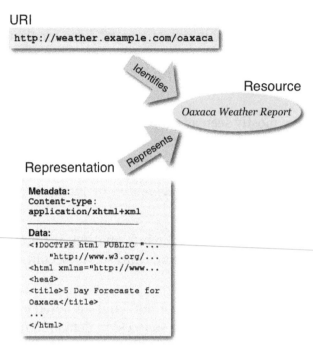

The URI-resource-representation story, from Jacobs and Walsh, eds. 2005, The Architecture of the World Wide Web

This can't be the whole story, since nothing in figure above looks anything like a weather report. What Web users experience in practice involves a further relationship, between a representation and what we might call a presentation:

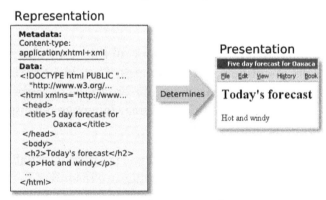

The representation-presentation story

There is important potential for variation in two aspects of the pictures above:

- Different representations may be available for the same resource, in at least four ways:

    1. Different technologies, manifested as different media types, for example GIF or JPG or PNG for an image, PDF or HTML or XHTML or TXT for structured text;

2. Different intended presentation platforms, for example desktop screen versus portable device;

3. In the case of text, different natural languages, for example the weather report in English or Spanish;

4. Different versions, either as a document evolves, or, more interestingly, because a resource is time-varying by nature, for example today's weather report.

- Different presentations may be determined by the same representation, ranging from simple changes in size, scale or fonts to changes in modality (digital display, print, even audio or braille) or even non-physical presentation for non-human consumption, for example, by the web crawlers used by search engines.

Figures above illustrate the static relationship between the various constituents of the URI story. There is also a dynamic story, which is where the Web comes in:

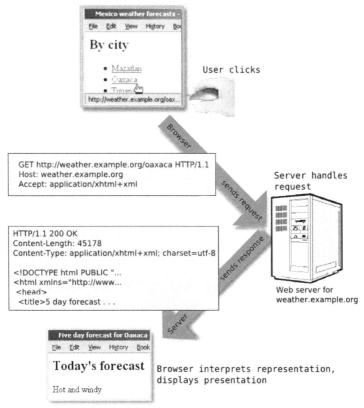

The HTTP request-response story

The underlying mechanism for accessing representations via the Web, the HyperText Transfer Protocol, or HTTP, provides for control over the first three kinds of variation. That is, by specifying parameters in the request from client to server to access a URI, the consumer can determine which representation the server responds with. In figure above, for example, we see the initial request includes an Accept header which specifies the XHTML media type, and that is indeed what the server sends back in the response.

The fourth kind of variation, variation of representation over time, is quite different, and leads on to some new and very interesting issues. In the cases of the Oaxaca weather report or the home page of your favourite online newspaper, it does seem right to say there is only one resource, despite the fact that the representations you can retrieve of such resources will vary a great deal from day to day.

There's an illuminating parallel here with the class of words in ordinary language which linguists call indexical, words such as this, here and tomorrow, as well as you and I. An indexical such as now has a single meaning but multiple interpretations. The meaning is something like "the time at which the utterance containing the word is made", and is the same for every use of the word. But the interpretation is, well, whatever time it happens to be when the word is used, and this of course changes all the time. More generally, the meaning of an indexical can be understood as a function from contexts (that is, contexts of utterance) to interpretations.

The situation with time-varying resources is just the same—indeed the gloss we gave to the examples above (yesterday's weather report, etc.) underlines this. Once the parallel is pointed out, it can be seen to apply to other, admittedly more specialised, URIs, such as http://localhost/... or file:///home/ht/...., which identify resources whose representations depend not (or not only) on when they are accessed, but also where.

To sum up: Although historically URIs were understood as a kind of Web-enabled file name, with a simple "URI points to web page" model, the move to separate conceptually the (stable) resource identified by a URI from its (potentially varied) representations was necessary to make sense of actual practice. The resource abstraction has gone on to provide powerful new functionality, a subject we will return to below.

Actual State of Play

The phrase "Web 2.0" means many different things, but one thing it is often used to refer to is a significant change in the way representations determine presentations. What a user sees on the screen today as a result of accessing a resource identified by a URI often depends as much if not more on running Javascript programs embedded in the retrieved (X)HTML representation, and on the results of other, behind-the-scenes, resource accesses, as it does on the (X)HTML itself. The coinage AJAX refers to this approach. For example, the presentation of a map which a user sees when using Google Maps is entirely constructed from images retrieved behind the scenes by the Javascript which makes up virtually all of the original representation as retrieved from the Google Maps URI.

As the proportion of a presentation that depends directly and declaratively on the initially retrieved representation diminishes, and the proportion based on local computation and representations retrieved behind the scenes increases, there is a kind of historical regression going on, which goes back to treating URIs instrumentally, as ways of moving data. What you can send and retrieve is all that matters, and the resource-representation distinction no longer seems to be doing useful work.

There are two things underlying this blurring of the resource-representation distinction in Web 2.0 usage:

- The kinds of flexibility provided by the kind of variation discussed above, in particular variation with respect to media type or natural language, are just not relevant to most behind-the-scenes web access;

- The distinction between the URI as such, and the rest of the request to the server, particularly with respect to explicit parameter specifications, is much less evident from the standpoint of the Javascript programmer. Both URI and parameters are things which have to be specified as part of a web request, and this encourages the viewpoint that taken together they identify what is wanted.

If behind-the-scenes URI usage tends to encourage a near-equation of resource and representation, other aspects of sophisticated Web 2.0 usage tend in the opposite direction. If the presentation experienced by a user varies independently of any user-controllable aspect of URI access, or evolves in response to user actions, the sense in which the URI visible at the top of the browser can be said to still 'identify' a representation which corresponds to that presentation has become attenuated almost to the point of vanishing.

If what you see depends on a cookie, you can't post a pointer to it in an email message, because the recipient won't have the right cookie. That's not necessarily a bad thing (you probably wouldn't want to be able to send an email message which lets someone into your bank account), but does act to diminish the connection between URI, resource and representation. If what you see depends on the IP address your request comes from or on a radio button value that doesn't show up as a URI parameter, then not only can you not point to it in email, but you can't (reliably) bookmark it, and Google doesn't index it, because its crawlers will never see it: crawlers don't tick boxes or share your IP address.

The original value proposition of the Web was produced by the network effect: for anything you were interested in, someone else somewhere was too, and they had produced a website about it, and search engines could find it for you.

But the Web as information appliance has evolved: not only is large amounts of web-delivered information not available via search engines, for the kind of reasons discussed above, even the famous page rank algorithm which launched Google's success doesn't work particularly well anymore, as the proportion of hand-authored pages has declined, and information access is increasingly controlled by a self-reinforcing feedback loop between Google and the big players in the information aggregation game, such as Wikipedia, Tripadvisor and MedicineNet: page ranking in Google today depends to a substantial extent on statistics over search terms and clickthroughs.

From the user perspective, a related phenomenon which threatens to further erode the centrality of the URI-resource connection is the use of the search entry field in browsers instead of the address field. Already in December of 2008, for example, 8 of the top 15 search terms reported by one service over the last five months were in fact the core parts of domain names (non-www., non-.com), and some actual domain names, such as myspace.com, yahoo.com and hotmail.com, were in the top fifty. Arguably the time when URIs were the primary currency of the Web is past, and they will disappear from view and consciousness for the vast majority of Web users in much the same way as the angle brackets and equal signs of raw HTML have done.

Emerging Future

As long ago as the mid-1990s, information scientists had taken the URI-resource-representation split to its logical conclusion: it was OK to create URIs for resources for which no representation existed yet (for example a planned but not-yet-drafted catalogue entry), or even for resources for which no (retrievable) representation could in principle ever exist (a particular physical book, or even its author). By the end of the 1990s, the generalisation of the resource concept was complete, and we find, in the defining document for URIs (since superseded, but without significant change in this regard):

> A resource can be anything that has identity. Familiar examples include an electronic document, an image, a service (e.g., "today's weather report for Los Angeles"), and a collection of other resources. Not all resources are network "retrievable"; e.g., human beings, corporations, and bound books in a library can also be considered resources.
>
> Berners-Lee, Fielding and Masinter 1998 RFC 2396, Uniform Resource Identifiers (URI): Generic Syntax

Since then the principle that a URI can be used to identify anything, that is, that there are few if any limits on what can "be a resource", has assumed more and more importance, particularly within one community, namely the participants in the so-called Semantic Web programme. This move is not just a theoretical possibility: there are more and more URIs appearing "in the wild" which do not identify images, reports, home pages or recordings, but rather people, places and even abstract relations.

But this in turn has lead to a problem. Time was, when you tried to access a URI, you either succeeded or failed. Success, as illustrated in figure above, and specifically signalled by the first line of the response message, HTTP/1.1 200 OK, meant a representation was coming next, and all was well. Failure meant the infamous "404 Not

Found" (whose official rendition is HTTP/1.1 404 Not Found) and no representation. Furthermore, success meant that the presentation determined by the representation you retrieved could be counted on to pretty well reproduce the resource identified by the URI itself. You could look at the image, or read the report, or listen to the recording, etc.

But what if we have a URI which identifies, let's say, not the Oaxaca weather report, but Oaxaca itself, that city in the Sierra Madre del Sur southeast of Mexico City? What should happen if we try to access that URI? If the access succeeds, the representation we get certainly won't reproduce Oaxaca very well: we won't be able to walk around in it, or smell the radishes if it happens to be the 23rd of December.

This is the point at which the word 'representation' is a problem. Surely we can retrieve some kind of representation of Oaxaca: a map, or a description, or a collection of aerial photographs. These are representations in the ordinary sense of the word, but not in the technical sense it is used when discussing Web architecture. Unfortunately, beyond pointing to the kind of easy examples we've used all along (a JPG is a good representation of an image, a HTML document can represent a report very well, an MP3 file can represent a recording pretty faithfully), it's hard to give a crisp definition of what 'representation' means in the technical sense, in order to justify the assertion that, for example, an image of Oaxaca does not 'represent' Oaxaca. The definition implied above, namely that a representation of a resource should determine a presentation that reproduces the resource for the perceiver, begs the question of what is meant by 'reproduce'. The Architecture of the World Wide Web, which is a systematic attempt to analyse the key properties on which the success of the Web depends, coined the term information resource for those resources for which a representation is possible. It defines the term in this way:

> The distinguishing characteristic of [information] resources is that all of their essential characteristics can be conveyed in a message.

This may seem like an academic question, one which indeed has important connections to both philosophy, particularly the philosophy of aesthetics, and to information science and the notorious question concerning "the nature of the work of art". But it has real practical consequences. There is real debate underway at the moment as to exactly what it means for a web server to return a 200 OK response code, and about exactly what kind of response is appropriate to a request for a URI which identifies a non-information resource. This question arises because, particularly in the context of Semantic Web applications, although no representation of the resource itself may be available, a representation of an information resource which describes that resource may be available. So, to go back to our example, there may be a representation available for a report on a visit to Oaxaca, or for a collection of images of Oaxaca, or even a set of formally-encoded propositions about Oaxaca. Such descriptions are often called metadata.

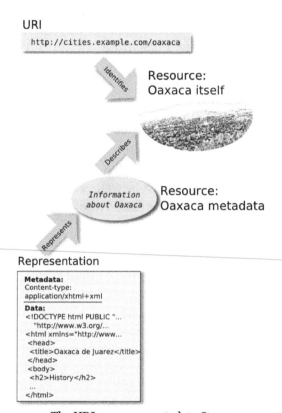

URI

`http://cities.example.com/oaxaca`

Identifies → Resource: Oaxaca itself

Describes →

Information about Oaxaca — Resource: Oaxaca metadata

Represents →

Representation

> **Metadata:**
> Content-type:
> application/xhtml+xml
>
> **Data:**
> `<!DOCTYPE html PUBLIC "...`
> `    "http://www.w3.org/...`
> `<html xmlns="http://www...`
> ` <head>`
> ` <title>Oaxaca de Juarez</title>`
> ` </head>`
> ` <body>`
> ` <h2>History</h2>`
> `   ...`
> `</html>`

The URI-resource-metadata Story

Generic Syntax

Each URI begins with a scheme name that refers to a specification for assigning identifiers within that scheme. As such, the URI syntax is a federated and extensible naming system wherein each scheme's specification may further restrict the syntax and semantics of identifiers using that scheme. The URI generic syntax is a superset of the syntax of all URI schemes. It was first defined in Request for Comments (RFC) 2396, published in August 1998, and finalized in RFC 3986, published in January 2005.

The *URI generic syntax* consists of a hierarchical sequence of five *components*:

```
URI = scheme:[//authority]path[?query][#fragment]
```

where the authority component divides into three *subcomponents*:

```
authority = [userinfo@]host[:port]
```

This is represented in a syntax diagram as:

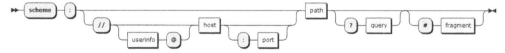

The URI comprises:

- A non-empty scheme component followed by a colon (:), consisting of a sequence of characters beginning with a letter and followed by any combination of letters, digits, plus (+), period (.), or hyphen (-). Although schemes are case-insensitive, the canonical form is lowercase and documents that specify schemes must do so with lowercase letters. Examples of popular schemes include http, https, ftp, mailto, file, data, and irc. URI schemes should be registered with the Internet Assigned Numbers Authority (IANA), although non-registered schemes are used in practice.

- An optional non-empty authority component preceded by two slashes (//), comprising:

  ◦ An optional userinfo subcomponent that may consist of a user name and an optional password preceded by a colon (:), followed by an at symbol (@). Use of the format username:password in the userinfo subcomponent is deprecated for security reasons. Applications should not render as clear text any data after the first colon (:) found within a userinfo subcomponent unless the data after the colon is the empty string (indicating no password).

  ◦ A non-empty host subcomponent, consisting of either a registered name (including but not limited to a hostname), or an IP address. IPv4 addresses must be in dot-decimal notation, and IPv6 addresses must be enclosed in brackets ([]).

  ◦ An optional port subcomponent preceded by a colon (:).

- A path component, consisting of a sequence of path segments separated by a slash (/). A path is always defined for a URI, though the defined path may be empty (zero length). A segment may also be empty, resulting in two consecutive slashes (//) in the path component. A path component may resemble or map exactly to a file system path, but does not always imply a relation to one. If an authority component is present, then the path component must either be empty or begin with a slash (/). If an authority component is absent, then the path cannot begin with an empty segment, that is with two slashes (//), as the following characters would be interpreted as an authority component. The final segment of the path may be referred to as a 'slug'.

Query delimiter	Example
Ampersand (&)	key1=value1&key2=value2
Semicolon (;)	key1=value1;key2=value2

- An optional query component preceded by a question mark (?), containing a query string of non-hierarchical data. Its syntax is not well defined, but by convention is most often a sequence of attribute–value pairs separated by a delimiter.

- An optional fragment component preceded by a hash (#). The fragment contains a fragment identifier providing direction to a secondary resource, such as a section heading in an article identified by the remainder of the URI. When the primary resource is an HTML document, the fragment is often an id attribute of a specific element, and web browsers will scroll this element into view.

Strings of data octets within a URI are represented as characters. Permitted characters within a URI are the ASCII characters for the lowercase and uppercase letters of the modern English alphabet, the Arabic numerals, hyphen, period, underscore, and tilde. Octets represented by any other character must be percent-encoded.

Of the ASCII character set, the characters : / ? # [ ] @ are reserved for use as delimiters of the generic URI components and must be percent-encoded — for example, %3F for a question mark. The characters ! $ & ' ( ) * + , ; = are permitted by generic URI syntax to be used unencoded in the user information, host, and path as delimiters. Additionally, : and @ may appear unencoded within the path, query, and fragment; and ? and / may appear unencoded as data within the query or fragment.

Examples

The following figure displays example URIs and their component parts.

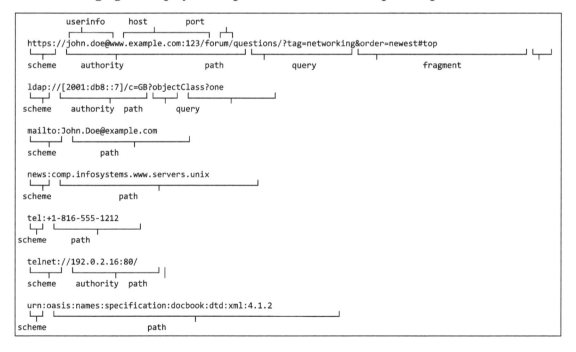

URI References

A *URI reference* is either a URI, or a *relative reference* when it does not begin with a scheme component followed by a colon (:). A path segment that contains a colon character (e.g., foo:bar) cannot be used as the first path segment of a relative reference if its path component does not begin with a slash (/), as it would be mistaken for a scheme component. Such a path segment must be preceded by a dot path segment (e.g., ./ foo:bar).

Web document markup languages frequently use URI references to point to other resources, such as external documents or specific portions of the same logical document:

- In html, the value of the src attribute of the img element provides a uri reference, as does the value of the href attribute of the a or link element;

- In xml, the system identifier appearing after the system keyword in a dtd is a fragmentless uri reference;

- In xslt, the value of the href attribute of the xsl:import element/instruction is a URI reference; likewise the first argument to the document() function.

Examples

```
https://example.com/path/resource.txt#fragment

//example.com/path/resource.txt

/path/resource.txt

path/resource.txt

/path/resource.txt

../resource.txt

./resource.txt

resource.txt

#fragment
```

URI Resolution

An *absolute URI* is a URI with no fragment component.

Resolving a URI reference against a *base URI* results in a *target URI*. This implies that the base URI exists and is an absolute URI. The base URI can be obtained, in order of precedence, from:

- The reference uri itself if it is a uri;

- The content of the representation;

- The entity encapsulating the representation;

- The uri used for the actual retrieval of the representation;

- The context of the application.

Examples

Within a representation with a well defined base URI of

http://a/b/c/d;p?q

a relative reference is resolved to its target URI as follows:

```
"g:h"      -> "g:h"
"g"        -> "http://a/b/c/g"
"./g"      -> "http://a/b/c/g"
"g/"       -> "http://a/b/c/g/"
"/g"       -> "http://a/g"
"//g"      -> "http://g"
"?y"       -> "http://a/b/c/d;p?y"
"g?y"      -> "http://a/b/c/g?y"
"#s"       -> "http://a/b/c/d;p?q#s"
"g#s"      -> "http://a/b/c/g#s"
"g?y#s"    -> "http://a/b/c/g?y#s"
";x"       -> "http://a/b/c/;x"
"g;x"      -> "http://a/b/c/g;x"
"g;x?y#s"  -> "http://a/b/c/g;x?y#s"
""         -> "http://a/b/c/d;p?q"
"."        -> "http://a/b/c/"
"./"       -> "http://a/b/c/"
".."       -> "http://a/b/"
"../"      -> "http://a/b/"
"../g"     -> "http://a/b/g"
"../.."    -> "http://a/"
"../../"   -> "http://a/"
"../../g"  -> "http://a/g"
```

Naming, Addressing, and Identifying Resources

URIs and URLs have a shared history. In 1994, Tim Berners-Lee's proposals for hypertext implicitly introduced the idea of a URL as a short string representing a resource that is the target of a hyperlink. At the time, people referred to it as a "hypertext name" or "document name".

Over the next three and a half years, as the World Wide Web's core technologies of HTML, HTTP, and web browsers developed, a need to distinguish a string that provided an address for a resource from a string that merely named a resource emerged. Although not yet formally defined, the term *Uniform Resource Locator* came to represent the former, and the more contentious *Uniform Resource Name* came to represent the latter.

During the debate over defining URLs and URNs it became evident that the two concepts embodied by the terms were merely aspects of the fundamental, overarching notion of resource *identification*. In June 1994, the IETF published Berners-Lee's RFC 1630: the first Request for Comments that acknowledged the existence of URLs and URNs, and, more importantly, defined a formal syntax for *Universal Resource Identifiers* — URL-like strings whose precise syntaxes and semantics depended on their schemes. In addition, this RFC attempted to summarize the syntaxes of URL schemes in use at the time. It also acknowledged, but did not standardize, the existence of relative URLs and fragment identifiers.

Refinement of Specifications

In December 1994, RFC 1738 formally defined relative and absolute URLs, refined the general URL syntax, defined how to resolve relative URLs to absolute form, and better enumerated the URL schemes then in use. The agreed definition and syntax of URNs had to wait until the publication of RFC 2141 in May 1997.

The publication of RFC 2396 in August 1998 saw the URI syntax become a separate specification and most of the parts of RFCs 1630 and 1738 relating to URIs and URLs in general were revised and expanded by the IETF. The new RFC changed the meaning of "U" in "URI" to "Uniform" from "Universal".

In December 1999, RFC 2732 provided a minor update to RFC 2396, allowing URIs to accommodate IPv6 addresses. A number of shortcomings discovered in the two specifications led to a community effort, coordinated by RFC 2396 co-author Roy Fielding, that culminated in the publication of RFC 3986 in January 2005. While obsoleting the prior standard, it did not render the details of existing URL schemes obsolete; RFC 1738 continues to govern such schemes except where otherwise superseded. RFC 2616 for example, refines the http scheme. Simultaneously, the IETF published the content of RFC 3986 as the full standard STD 66, reflecting the establishment of the URI generic syntax as an official Internet protocol.

In 2001, the W3C's Technical Architecture Group (TAG) published a guide to best practices and canonical URIs for publishing multiple versions of a given resource. For example, content might differ by language or by size to adjust for capacity or settings of the device used to access that content.

In August 2002, RFC 3305 pointed out that the term "URL" had, despite widespread public use, faded into near obsolescence, and serves only as a reminder that some URIs act as addresses by having schemes implying network accessibility, regardless of any such actual use. As URI-based standards such as Resource Description Framework make evident, resource identification need not suggest the retrieval of resource representations over the Internet, nor need they imply network-based resources at all.

The Semantic Web uses the HTTP URI scheme to identify both documents and concepts in the real world, a distinction which has caused confusion as to how to distinguish the two. The TAG published an e-mail in 2005 on how to solve the problem, which became known as the *httpRange-14 resolution*. The W3C subsequently published an Interest Group Note titled *Cool URIs for the Semantic Web*, which explained the use of content negotiation and the HTTP 303 response code for redirections in more detail.

Relation to XML Namespaces

In XML, a namespace is an abstract domain to which a collection of element and attribute names can be assigned. The namespace name is a character string which must adhere to the generic URI syntax. However, the name is generally not considered to be a URI, because the URI specification bases the decision not only on lexical components, but also on their intended use. A namespace name does not necessarily imply any of the semantics of URI schemes; for example, a namespace name beginning with *http:* may have no connotation to the use of the HTTP.

Originally, the namespace name could match the syntax of any non-empty URI reference, but the use of relative URI references was deprecated by the W3C. A separate W3C specification for namespaces in XML 1.1 permits internationalized resource identifier (IRI) references to serve as the basis for namespace names in addition to URI references.

URL

A URL (Uniform Resource Locator) is a form of URI and is a standardized naming convention for addressing documents accessible over the Internet and Intranet. An example of a URL is https://www.computerhope.com/, which is the URL for the Computer Hope website.

http:// or https://

The "http" stands for HyperText Transfer Protocol and is what enables the browser to know what protocol it is going to use to access the information specified in the domain. An "https" protocol is short for "Hypertext Transfer Protocol Secure" and indicates that information transmitted over HTTP is encrypted and secure. After the http or https is the colon (:) and two forward slashes (//) that separate the protocol from the remainder of the URL.

Tip: A URL is not explicit to a HTTP or HTTPS addresses; FTP, TFTP, Telnet, and other addresses are also considered URLs and may not follow the same syntax as our example.

www

Next, "www" stands for World Wide Web and is used to distinguish the content. This portion of the URL is not required and many times can be left out. For example, typing "http://computerhope.com" would still get you to the Computer Hope web page. This portion of the address can also be substituted for an important sub page known as a subdomain.

computerhope.com

Next, "computerhope.com" is the domain name for the website. The last portion of the domain is known as the domain suffix, or TLD, and is used to identify the type or location of the website. For example, ".com" is short for commercial, ".org" is short for an organization, and ".co.uk" is the United Kingdom. There are dozens of other domain suffixes available. To get a domain, you would register the name through a domain registrar.

/jargon/u/

Next, the "jargon" and "u" portions of the above URL are the directories of where on the server the web page is located. In this example, the web page is two directories deep, so if you were trying to find the file on the server, it would be in the /public_html/jargon/u directory. With most servers, the public_html directory is the default directory containing the HTML files.

url.htm

Finally, url.htm is the actual web page on the domain you're viewing. The trailing .htm is the file extension of the web page that indicates the file is an HTML file. Other common file extensions on the Internet include .html, .php, .asp, .cgi, .xml, .jpg, and .gif. Each of these file extensions performs a different function, just like all the different types of files on your computer.

Characters not allowed in a URL

Most people realize that a space is not allowed in a URL. However, it is also important to realize, as documented in RFC 1738, the URL string can only contain alphanumeric characters and the !$-_+*'(), characters. Any other characters that are needed in the URL must be encoded.

Understanding more Complex URLs and Parameters

When a URL points to a script that performs additional functions, such as a search engine pointing to a search results page, additional information (parameters) is added to the end of the URL. Below is additional information about a URL that points to the Computer Hope Search page, with the search query of "example search".

> ../../cgi-bin/search.cgi?q=example%20search

In this URL, the script file being pointed to is search.cgi in the cgi-bin directory. Because this file ends with .cgi, it is assumed to be a Perl script.

After the script file name is a ? (question mark). The question mark in a URL separates the URL from all the parameters or variables that are being sent to the script. In the above example, the parameter being sent is q=example%20search. The "q" is a variable name, and the "example%20search" is the value being sent to that variable. Because no spaces are allowed in a URL, the space has been encoded as %20. In many scripts, a + (plus) is also used to represent a space.

In our example, because there is a variable the script would use it as it is executed. Scripts are also not limited to only one variable. If the script needs multiple variables, each variable can be separated with an & (ampersand) as shown in the example below.

> ../../cgi-bin/search.cgi?q=example%20search&example=test

In the above example, there are two different variables. The "q" variable equals "example search" and the "example" variable equals "test". If the script was looking for an example variable, it could be processed and perform an additional feature.

Location of URL

A URL is located at the top of the browser window in the address bar or omnibox depending on your browser window. On desktop computers and laptop, unless your browser is being displayed in full screen the URL is always visible. In most smartphone and tablet browsers, the address bar containing the URL will disappear as you scroll down and only show the domain when visible. When the address bar is not visible scrolling up on the page will show the address bar and if only the domain is shown tapping on the address bar shows the full address.

Internationalized URL

Internet users are distributed throughout the world using a wide variety of languages and alphabets and expect to be able to create URLs in their own local alphabets. An Internationalized Resource Identifier (IRI) is a form of URL that includes Unicode characters. All modern browsers support IRIs. The parts of the URL requiring special treatment for different alphabets are the domain name and path.

The domain name in the IRI is known as an Internationalized Domain Name (IDN). Web and Internet software automatically convert the domain name into punycode usable by the Domain Name System; for example, the Chinese URL http://例子.卷筒纸 becomes http://xn--fsquo0a.xn--3lr804guic/. The xn-- indicates that the character was not originally ASCII.

The URL path name can also be specified by the user in the local writing system. If not already encoded, it is converted to UTF-8, and any characters not part of the basic URL character set are escaped as hexadecimal using percent-encoding; for example, the Japanese URL http://example.com/引き割り.html becomes http://example.com/%E5%BC%95%E3%81%8D%E5%89%B2%E3%82%8A.html. The target computer decodes the address and displays the page.

Protocol-relative URLs

Protocol-relative links (PRL), also known as protocol-relative URLs (PRURL), are URLs that have no protocol specified. For example, //example.com will use the protocol of the current page, either HTTP or HTTPS.

URN

A Uniform Resource Name (URN) is a Uniform Resource Identifier (URI) that uses the urn scheme.

URNs were originally conceived to be part of a three-part information architecture for the Internet, along with Uniform Resource Locators (URLs) and Uniform Resource Characteristics (URCs), a metadata framework. As described in the 1994 RFC 1737,, and later in the 1997 RFC 2141 , URNs were distinguished from URLs, which identify resources by specifying their locations in the context of a particular access protocol, such as HTTP or FTP. In contrast, URNs were conceived as persistent, location-independent identifiers assigned within defined namespaces, typically by an authority responsible for the namespace, so that they are globally unique and persistent over long periods of time, even after the resource which they identify ceases to exist or becomes unavailable.

URCs never progressed past the conceptual stage, and other technologies such as the Resource Description Framework later took their place. Since RFC 3986 in 2005, use of the terms "Uniform Resource Name" and "Uniform Resource Locator" has been deprecated in technical standards in favor of the term Uniform Resource Identifier (URI), which encompasses both, a view proposed in 2001 by a joint working group between the World Wide Web Consortium (W3C) and Internet Engineering Task Force (IETF).

A URI is a string of characters used to identify a name or resource. URIs are used in many Internet protocols to refer to and access information resources. URI schemes include the familiar http, as well as hundreds of others.

In the "contemporary view", as it is called, all URIs identify or name resources, perhaps uniquely and persistently, with some of them also being "locators" which are resolvable in conjunction with a specified protocol to a representation of the resources.

Other URIs are not locators and are not necessarily resolvable within the bounds of the systems where they are found. These URIs may serve as names or identifiers of resources. Since resources can move, opaque identifiers which *are not* locators and are not bound to particular locations are arguably more likely than identifiers which *are* locators to remain unique and persistent over time. But whether a URI is resolvable depends on many operational and practical details, irrespective of whether it is called a "name" or a "locator". In the contemporary view, there is no bright line between "names" and "locators".

In accord with this way of thinking, the distinction between Uniform Resource *Names* and Uniform Resource *Locators* is now no longer used in formal Internet Engineering Task Force technical standards, though the latter term, URL, is still in wide informal use.

The term "URN" continues now as one of more than a hundred URI "schemes", urn:, paralleling http:, ftp:, and so forth. URIs of the urn: scheme are not locators, are not required to be associated with a particular protocol or access method, and need not be resolvable. They should be assigned by a procedure which provides some assurance that they will remain unique and identify the same resource persistently over a prolonged period. Some namespaces under the urn: scheme, such as urn:uuid: assign identifiers in a manner which does not require a registration authority, but most of them do. A typical URN namespace is urn:isbn, for International Standard Book Numbers. This view is continued in the 2017 RFC 8141 .

There are other URI schemes, such as tag:, info:, and ni: which are similar to the urn: scheme in not being locators and not being associated with particular resolution or access protocols.

Syntax

The syntax of a urn: scheme URI is represented in the augmented Backus–Naur form as:

```
namestring     = assigned-name

                 [ rq-components ]

                 [ "#" f-component ]

assigned-name = "urn" ":" NID ":" NSS

NID            = (alphanum) 0*30(ldh) (alphanum)
```

```
ldh            = alphanum / "-"

NSS            = pchar *(pchar / "/")

rq-components = [ "?+" r-component ]

               [ "?=" q-component ]

r-component    = pchar *( pchar / "/" / "?" )

q-component    = pchar *( pchar / "/" / "?" )

f-component    = fragment
```

or, in the form of a syntax diagram, as:

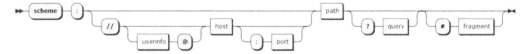

- The leading scheme (urn:) is case-insensitive.

- <NID> is the namespace identifier, and may include letters, digits, and -.

- The NID is followed by the namespace-specific string <NSS>, the interpretation of which depends on the specified namespace. The NSS may contain ASCII letters and digits, and many punctuation and special characters. Disallowed ASCII and Unicode characters may be included if percent-encoded.

In 2017 the syntax for URNs was updated as follows:

- The slash character (/) is now allowed in the NSS to represent names containing slashes from non-URN identifier systems.

- The q-component was added to enable passing of parameters to named resources.

- The r-component was added to enable passing of parameters to resolvers. However, the updated specification notes that the r-component should not be used until its semantics are defined via further standardization.

Namespaces

In order to ensure the global uniqueness of URN namespaces, their identifiers (NIDs) are required to be registered with the IANA. Registered namespaces may be "formal" or "informal". An exception to the registration requirement was formerly made for "experimental namespaces", since rescinded by RFC 8141.

Formal

Approximately sixty formal URN namespace identifiers have been registered. These are namespaces where Internet users are expected to benefit from their publication, and are subject to several restrictions. They must:

- Not be an already-registered NID

- Not start with urn-

- Be more than two letters long

- Not start with XY-, where XY is any combination of two ASCII letters

- Not start with x-

Informal

Informal namespaces are registered with IANA and assigned a number sequence (chosen by IANA on a first-come-first-served basis) as an identifier, in the format

> "urn-" <number>

Informal namespaces are fully fledged URN namespaces and can be registered in global registration services.

Experimental

An exception to the registration requirement was formerly made for "experimental namespaces". However, following the deprecation of the "X-" notation for new identifier names , RFC 8141 did away with experimental URN namespaces, indicating a preference for use of the urn:example namespace where appropriate.

Difference Between URLs and URIs

There are many classic tech debates, and the question of what to formally call web addresses is one of the most nuanced. The way this normally manifests is someone asks for the "URL" to put into his or her browser, and someone perks up with,

The response to this correction can range from quietly thinking this person needs to get out more, to agreeing indifferently via shoulder shrug, to removing the safety clasp on a Katana. This page hopes to serve as a simple, one page summary for navigating the subtleties of this debate.

URI, URL, URN

As the image above indicates, there are three distinct components at play here. It's usually best to go to the source when discussing matters like these, so here's an excerpt from Tim Berners-Lee, et. al. in rfc 3986: uniform resource identifier (uri): generic syntax:

A Uniform Resource Identifier (URI) is a compact sequence of characters that identifies an abstract or physical resource.

A URI can be further classified as a locator, a name, or both. The term "Uniform Resource Locator" (URL) refers to the subset of URIs that, in addition to identifying a resource, provides a means of locating the resource by describing its primary access mechanism (e.g., its network "location").

One can classify URIs as locators (URLs), or as names (URNs), or as both. A Uniform Resource Name (URN) functions like a person's name, while a Uniform Resource Locator (URL) resembles that person's street address. In other words: the URN defines an item's identity, while the URL provides a method for finding it.

- First of all a URL is a type of URI. So if someone tells you that a URL is not a URI, he's wrong. But that doesn't mean all URIs are URLs. All butterflies fly, but not everything that flies is a butterfly.

- The part that makes a URI a URL is the inclusion of the "access mechanism", or "network location", e.g. http:// or ftp://.

- The URN is the "globally unique" part of the identification; it's a unique name.

So let's look at some examples of URIs—again from the RFC:

- ftp://ftp.is.co.za/rfc/rfc1808.txt (also a URL because of the protocol)

- http://www.ietf.org/rfc/rfc2396.txt (also a URL because of the protocol)

- ldap://[2001:db8::7]/c=GB?objectClass?one (also a URL because of the protocol)

- mailto:John.Doe@example.com (also a URL because of the protocol)

- news:comp.infosystems.www.servers.unix (also a URL because of the protocol)

- tel:+1-816-555-1212

- telnet://192.0.2.16:80/ (also a URL because of the protocol)

- urn:oasis:names:specification:docbook:dtd:xml:4.1.2

Those are all URIs, and some of them are URLs. Which are URLs? The ones that show you how to get to them. Again, the name vs. address analogy serves well.

More Proper Term when Referring to Web Addresses

Based on the dozen or so articles and RFCs one read while researching this part, one would say that depends on a very simple thing: whether you give the full thing or just a piece.

Well, because we often use URIs in forms that don't technically qualify as a URL. For example, you might be told that a file you need is located at files.hp.com. That's a URI, not a URL—and that system might very well respond to many protocols over many ports.

If you go to http://files.hp.com you could conceivably get completely different content than if you go to ftp://files.hp.com. And this type of thing is only getting more common. Think of all the different services that live on the various Google domains.

So, if you use URI you'll always be technically correct, and if you use URL you might not be.

But if you definitely dealing with an actual full URL, then "URL" is most accurate because it's most specific. Humans are technically African apes, and dogs are mammals, but we rightly call them humans and dogs, respectively. And if you're an American from San Francisco, and you meet someone from Sydney while in Boston, you wouldn't say you're from Earth, or from the United States. You'd say California, or—even better— San Francisco.

So until something changes, URI is best used when you're referring to a resource just by its name or some other fragment. And when you're giving both the name of a resource and the method of accessing it (like a full URL), it's best to call that a **URL**.

In Short:

1. URIs are *identifiers*, and that can mean name, location, or both.

2. All URNs and URLs are URIs, but the opposite is not true.

3. The part that makes something a URL is the combination of the name and an access method, such as https://, or mailto:.

4. All these bits are URIs, so saying that is always technically accurate, but if you are discussing something that's both a full URL and a URI (which all URLs are), it's best to call it a "URL" because it's more specific.

HTTP

Short for Hypertext Transfer Protocol, HTTP is a set of standards that allow users of the World Wide Web to exchange information found on web pages. When accessing any web page entering http:// in front of the address tells the browser to communicate over HTTP. For example, the URL for Computer Hope is https://www.computerhope.com. Today's browsers no longer require HTTP in front of the URL since it is the default method of communication. However, it is kept in browsers because of the need to separate protocols such as FTP. Below are a few of the major facts on HTTP.

- The term HTTP was coined by Ted Nelson.

- The standard port for HTTP connections is port 80.

- HTTP/0.9 was the first version of the HTTP, and was introduced in 1991.

- HTTP/1.0 is specified in RFC 1945, and was introduced in 1996.

- HTTP/1.1 is specified in RFC 2616, and was officially released in January 1997.

HTTPS

Short for Hypertext Transfer Protocol Secure, HTTPS is a protocol which uses HTTP on a connection encrypted by transport-layer security. HTTPS is used to protect transmitted data from eavesdropping. It is the default protocol for conducting financial transactions on the web, and can protect a website's users from censorship by a government or an ISP.

- HTTPS uses port 443 to transfer its information.

- HTTPS is first used in HTTP/1.1 and is defined in RFC 2616.

HTTP Status Codes

Below is a listing of HTTP status codes currently defined by Computer Hope. These codes enable a client accessing another computer or device over HTTP to know how to proceed or not proceed. For example, 404 tells the browser the request does not exist on the server.

404Below is a listing of HTTP status codes currently defined by Computer Hope. These codes enable a client accessing another computer or device over HTTP to know how to proceed or not proceed. For example, 404 tells the browser the request does not exist on the server.

1xx - 2xx	3xx - 4xx	5xx
100 (Continue)	301 (Moved permanently)	500 (Internal server error)
101 (Switch protocols)	302 (Moved temporarily)	501 (Not Implemented)
102 (Processing)	304 (Loaded Cached copy)	502 (Bad gateway)
200 (Success)	307 (Internal redirect)	503 (Service unavailable)
201 (Fulfilled)	400 (Bad request)	504 (Gateway timeout)
202 (Accepted)	401 (Authorization required)	505 (HTTP version not supported)
204 (No content)	402 (Payment required)	506 (Variant also negotiates)
205 (Reset content)	403 (Forbidden)	507 (Insufficient storage)
206 (Partial content)	404 (Not found)	510 (Not extended)
207 (Multi-Status)	405 (Method not allowed)	
	406 (Not acceptable)	
	407 (Proxy authentication required)	
	408 (Request timeout)	
	409 (Conflict)	
	410 (Gone)	
	411 (Length required)	
	412 (Precondition failed)	
	413 (Request entity too large)	
	414 (Request URI too large)	
	415 (Unsupported media type)	
	416 (Request range not satisfiable)	
	417 (Expectation failed)	
	422 (Unprocessable entity)	
	423 (Locked)	
	424 (Failed dependency)	

Overall Operation

The HTTP protocol is a request/response protocol. A client sends a request to the server in the form of a request method, URI, and protocol version, followed by a MIME-like message containing request modifiers, client information, and possible body content over a connection with a server. The server responds with a status line, including the message's protocol version and a success or error code, followed by a MIME-like message containing server information, entity metainformation, and possible entity-body content.

Most HTTP communication is initiated by a user agent and consists of a request to be applied to a resource on some origin server. In the simplest case, this may be accomplished via a single connection (v) between the user agent (UA) and the origin server (O).

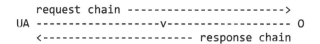

```
                  request chain ----------------------->
           UA ------------------v------------------ O
              <--------------------- response chain
```

A more complicated situation occurs when one or more intermediaries are present in the request/response chain. There are three common forms of intermediary: proxy, gateway, and tunnel. A proxy is a forwarding agent, receiving requests for a URI in its absolute form, rewriting all or part of the message, and forwarding the reformatted request toward the server identified by the URI. A gateway is a receiving agent, acting as a layer above some other server(s) and, if necessary, translating the requests to the underlying server's protocol. A tunnel acts as a relay point between two connections without changing the messages; tunnels are used when the communication needs to pass through an intermediary (such as a firewall) even when the intermediary cannot understand the contents of the messages.

```
      request chain --------------------------------------->
UA -----v----- A -----v----- B -----v----- C -----v----- O
      <--------------------------------- response chain
```

The figure above shows three intermediaries (A, B, and C) between the user agent and origin server. A request or response message that travels the whole chain will pass through four separate connections. This distinction is important because some HTTP communication options may apply only to the connection with the nearest, non-tunnel neighbor, only to the end-points of the chain, or to all connections along the chain. Although the diagram is linear, each participant may be engaged in multiple, simultaneous communications. For example, B may be receiving requests from many clients other than A, and/or forwarding requests to servers other than C, at the same time that it is handling A's request.

Any party to the communication which is not acting as a tunnel may employ an internal cache for handling requests. The effect of a cache is that the request/response chain is shortened if one of the participants along the chain has a cached response applicable to that request. The following illustrates the resulting chain if B has a cached copy of an earlier response from O (via C) for a request which has not been cached by UA or A.

```
      request chain ---------->
UA -----v----- A -----v----- B - - - - - - C - - - - - - O
      <--------- response chain
```

Not all responses are usefully cacheable, and some requests may contain modifiers which place special requirements on cache behavior. In fact, there are a wide variety of architectures and configurations of caches and proxies currently being experimented with or deployed across the World Wide Web. These systems include national hierarchies of proxy caches to save transoceanic bandwidth, systems that broadcast or multicast cache entries, organizations that distribute subsets of cached data via CD-ROM, and so on. HTTP systems are used in corporate intranets over high-bandwidth links, and for access via PDAs with low-power radio links and intermittent connectivity. The goal of HTTP/1.1 is to support the wide diversity of configurations already deployed while introducing protocol constructs that meet the needs of those who build web applications that require high reliability and, failing that, at least reliable indications of failure.

HTTP communication usually takes place over TCP/IP connections. The default port is TCP 80, but other ports can be used. This does not preclude HTTP from being implemented on top of any other protocol on the Internet, or on other networks. HTTP only presumes a reliable transport; any protocol that provides such guarantees can be used; the mapping of the HTTP/1.1 request and response structures onto the transport data units of the protocol in question is outside the scope of this specification.

In HTTP/1.0, most implementations used a new connection for each request/response exchange. In HTTP/1.1, a connection may be used for one or more request/response exchanges, although connections may be closed for a variety of reasons.

Issues with HTTP

Messages transmitted over HTTP can fail to be delivered successfully for several reasons:

- User error

- Malfunction of the web browser or web server

- Errors in the creation of web pages

- Temporary network glitches

When these failures occur, the protocol captures the cause of the failure (if possible) and reports an error code back to the browser called an HTTP status line/code. Errors begin with a certain number to indicate what kind of error it is.

For example, 4xx errors indicate that the request for the page can not be completed properly or that the request contains incorrect syntax. As an example, 404 errors means that the page can not be found; some websites even have some fun custom 404 error pages.

CGI (Common Gateway Interface) is a standard way of running programs from a Web server. Often, CGI programs are used to generate pages dynamically or to perform some other action when someone fills out an HTML form and clicks the submit button. AOLserver provides full support for CGI v1.1.

Basically, CGI works like this:

A reader sends a URL that causes the AOLserver to use CGI to run a program. The AOLserver passes input from the reader to the program and output from the program back to the reader. CGI acts as a "gateway" between the AOLserver and the program you write.

The program run by CGI can be any type of executable file on the server platform. For example, you can use C, C++, Perl, Unix shell scripts, Fortran, or any other compiled or interpreted language. You can also use Tcl scripts with CGI, though the extensions to Tcl described in the *AOLserver Tcl Developer's Guide* are not available through CGI.

With AOLserver, you have the option of using the embedded Tcl and C interfaces instead of CGI. Typically, the Tcl and C interfaces provide better performance than CGI.

You may want to use CGI for existing, shareware, or freeware programs that use the standard CGI input, output, and environment variables. Since CGI is a standard interface used by many Web servers, there are lots of example programs and function libraries available on the World Wide Web and by ftp. It describes the interface and points you to locations where you can download examples.

Here is a diagram of how a CGI program runs:

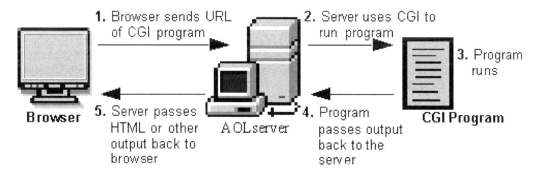

For example, suppose you have a form that lets people comment on your Web pages. You want the comments emailed to you and you want to automatically generate a page and send it back to your reader.

1. The reader fills out your form and clicks the "Submit" button. The <FORM> tag in your page might look like this:

    ```
    <FORM METHOD="POST" ACTION="/cgi-bin/myprog">
    ```

    The METHOD controls how the information typed into the form is passed to your program. It can be "GET" or "POST". The ACTION determines which program should be run.

Other ways for a reader to run a program are by providing a direct link to the program without allowing the reader to supply any variables through a form, or by using the <ISINDEX> tag.

2. When AOLserver gets a request for a URL that maps to a CGI directory or a CGI file extension it starts a separate process and runs the program within that process. The AOLserver also sets up a number of environment variables within that process. These environment variables include some standard CGI variables, and optionally any variables you define in the configuration file for this type of program.

3. The program runs. The program can be any type of executable program. For example, you can use C, C++, Perl, Unix shell scripts, or Fortran.

   In this example, the program takes the comments from the form as input and sends them to you as email. If the form method is "GET", it gets the input from an environment variable. If the form method is "POST", it gets the input from standard input. It also assembles a HTML page and sends it to standard output.

4. Any information the program passes to standard output is automatically sent to the AOLserver when the program finishes running.

5. The server adds any header information needed to identify the output and sends it back to the reader's browser, which displays the output.

References

- Berners-Lee, Tim (21 March 1994). "Uniform Resource Locators (URL): A Syntax for the Expression of Access Information of Objects on the Network". World Wide Web Consortium. Retrieved 13 September 2015.

- Website-architecture-30409: techopedia.com, Retrieved 11 July 2018

- Web-application-architecture: stackify.com, Retrieved 19 June 2018

- Hansen, T.; Hardie, T. (June 2015). Thaler, D., ed. "Guidelines and Registration Procedures for URI Schemes". Internet Engineering Task Force. ISSN 2070-1721.

- 3-types-of-web-application-architecture: mobidev.biz, Retrieved 26 May 2018

- Web-browser-functions-of-web-browser: msatechnosoft.in, Retrieved 30 March 2018

- Hypertext-transfer-protocol-817944: lifewire.com, Retrieved 10 March 2018

E-commerce

The process of buying or selling or making any transaction online falls under the wide spectrum of e-commerce. The diverse aspects of e-commerce such as billing settlement plan, digital currency, electronic trading, etc. have been thoroughly discussed in this chapter.

E-commerce electronic commerce or EC is the buying and selling of goods and services, or the transmitting of funds or data, over an electronic network, primarily the internet. These business transactions occur either as business-to-business, business-to-consumer, consumer-to-consumer or consumer-to-business.

The terms e-commerce and e-business are often used interchangeably. The term e-tail is also sometimes used in reference to transactional processes for online shopping.

The beginnings of e-commerce can be traced to the 1960s, when businesses started using Electronic Data Interchange (EDI) to share business documents with other companies. In 1979, the American National Standards Institute developed ASC X12 as a universal standard for businesses to share documents through electronic networks.

After the number of individual users sharing electronic documents with each other grew in the 1980s, the rise of eBay and Amazon in the 1990s revolutionized the e-commerce industry. Consumers can now purchase endless amounts of items online, from e-tailers, from typical brick-and-mortar stores with e-commerce capabilities, and from one another.

Differences between e-commerce and e-business

E-commerce is often confused with e-business, although they have nothing to do with one another.

E-commerce only refers to the goods and services transaction between a seller and a consumer, whereas e-business refers to the complete process necessary to manage an online business.

Within e-business we can find, for example:

- Inbound marketing.
- Sales promotions.
- Stock control.
- SEO.
- Email marketing.

The e-business concept is wider than the e-commerce one and e-commerce is actually a part of e-business since it is a type of business model.

Types of e-commerce

The e-commerce field is really large and there are a lot of different models.

We are going to use two categories:

- A general one based on who the buyers and sellers are.
- Another one with different e-commerce "models".

1. According to the commercial profile

Each business focuses on a type of client, and depending on who they are, we can classify them:

- B2B (Business-to-Business): businesses whose clients are also businesses or organizations. For example, we could think about a construction materials company selling its products to arquitects and interior designers.
- B2C (Business-to-Consumer): businesses that sell their products or services directly to the consumer. This is the usual type and there are thousands of examples of clothes, shoes or electronics stores.
- C2B (Consumer-to-Business): sites in which consumers offer products or services and businesses bid on them. We are talking about the traditional websites for freelancers such as Freelancer, Twago, Nubelo or Adtriboo.

- C2C (Consumer-to-Consumer): businesses that facilitate the selling of products amongst consumers. The clearest example is eBay or any other second hand website.

In addition to these types of electronic commerce, there are other popular types such as G2C (Goverment-to-Consumer), C2G (Consumer-to-Goverment) or B2E (Business-to-Employer).

E-commerce is more than a simply transaction in a store.

2. According to the Business Model

The online sector is still not very mature. Technology is always changing and the new online businesses that are popping up are trying to meet the new needs being created.

Depending on how the income is generated or how the exchange between buyer and seller takes place, they can be divided into:

- Online shop with its own products: The first idea that came to you when you heard about e-commerce. They have the same characteristics as a physical store, but they in an online version. For example: tauntonleisure.com

- Dropshipping: For the client, everything looks like a normal e-commerce shop. The difference is that it is not the e-commerce shop seller who sends the product, but rather a third party.

- Affiliate e-commerce: A step further back in the buying process we can find affiliate businesses. In this case, not only does the shop not send the product, the purchase completion is not even carried out via its platform. What these businesses do is sending clients to different shops in exchange for a commission that they receive once the purchase is completed. Affiliation is very common with Amazon. For example: Biodegradable.es.

- Membership: This type of e-commerce aims for recurring purchases. They achieve this by using periodic subscriptions (weekly, monthly, bimonthly, etc.). These types of memberships are in currently in fashion with the so-called "surprise boxes". They are boxes that are sent each month with different products, for example, a monthly box with different craft beers. Instead of selling the product just once, the shops offer the option of receiving it with a predetermined frequency. For example: Manolitoandco.com.

- Marketplace: A marketplace is a department store. It is a website where different sellers offer their products from one or more sectors. Amazon is also an example of a marketplace. Although it also works as a normal e-commerce shop, everyone can sell using the platform in exchange for a big commission for Mr. Bezos.

- Services: An e-commerce business doesn't only have to be about selling products. Training, counselling, mentoring, or any other exchange of time for money is another viable option in order to start a business without risks.

Steps to Create an e-commerce

1. The idea

Do you already have an idea or are you starting from scratch? If you don't have a clear idea, there are several strategies for finding possible opportunities.

They are all about opening your mind and being attentive to observe every daily situation from an entrepreneurial point of view.

If you are walking around, have a look at every single physical business you see and think if its products could be sold on the Internet, if they aren't already.

What things do people normally complain about?

Or even better, don't use your walks to think about this, but rather establish a day and time to go out and look for ideas.

Look at what people wear and how they behave. Observe and write down any ideas you may think of—without filtering them.

Always think about solving people's problems and bear in mind that the entrepreneur's mind needs training. The first days when you start going to the gym make your body sore until it becomes accustomed. This is no different.

But the most important thing is that you have this idea clearly in mind: don't sell products, solve problems.

2. Analyze the idea

The second step is about narrowing down the first list of ideas until you have just a few.

These are the e-commerce ideas you will analyze:

- Value proposition: What is its value? Which need does it meet?
- Market: Is it a new product? Is it an already existing product with new functionalities?
- Competitors: Who is already meeting the needs that you have detected? Could you improve upon it?
- Demand: Is the problem that you are going to solve widespread enough to create sufficient demand? Check to see how many people are looking for it on Google.

- Difficulties: Make a list of other challenges that you may think of (technical problems, competitors, threats, etc.)

An excellent way of analyzing ideas is by using this basic entrepreneur's tool: SWOT.

SWOT is a matrix that, from an internal an external point of view, analyzes the Strengths, Weaknesses, Opportunities, and Threats of your idea.

Definitions of SWOTs

	Helpful to achieving the objective	Harmful to achieving the objective
Internal (attributes of the organization)	Strengths	Weaknesses
External (attributes of the environment)	Opportunities	Threats

3. Strategy

In the UK, 167.717 new companies have been registered from January to March, but most of them start out in a very disorganized way without designing any type of strategy.

And be sure that clearly knowing where to go and by which means will determine the success of your e-commerce shop.

You can ask yourself the following questions:

- How is your ideal client going to learn about you?

- Why are they going to prefer you to your competitors?

- Are you going to be cheaper?

- What defines your clients? What characteristics do they have in common?

- What are your business goals? How are you going to grow?

In order to define your e-commerce strategy we are going to use a business model canvas.

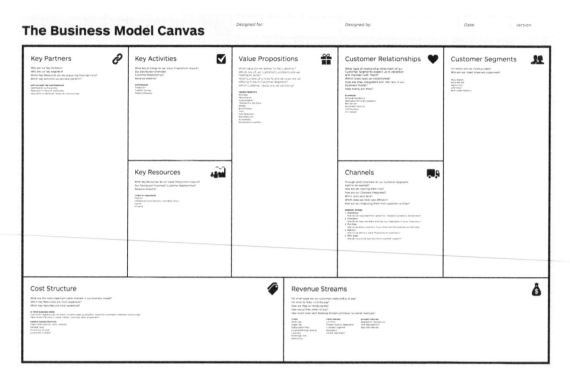

This template allows us to quickly and easily summarize the keys of a business. Spending the time to fill in these 9 boxes will help you find out what's important for your idea and how to carry it out.

4. Plan of action

Up to this moment you have only defined general ideas and goals. It is in this fourth step where you need to be more precise and define specific actions in line with the established strategy.

We'll give you a few hints:

- Name: This is one of the biggest headaches at the beginning. Our advice is to follow basic guidelines, such as to making it short, easy to pronounce, and that it is available for the .com domain and main social networks.

- Hosting: An e-commerce business needs a host.

- Corporative identity: Here we are not only talking about the colors or the logo but about the values you want to transmit—the real brand essence.

- Website: Who is going to build your website? If it is not going to be you, you will need someone to have it done or to advise you. Check out the different options depending on your business model: PrestaShop, WordPress, Shopify, etc.

- Visibility: We mention it last here, but this is actually the most important and most forgotten part of the plan of action. Most entrepreneurs make huge efforts to have a good product and a good website to sell it, but they don't think how to reach the client.

Advantages and Disadvantages of Starting up an e-commerce Shop

The advantages of e-commerce compared to traditional commerce are really powerful.

Advantages

1. More clients: There is no local store or company with sufficient offices in different cities that compares with e-commerce's reach. The possibility of selling and buying from any part of the world expands the target public and allows the company to gain more clients.

2. No schedule: E-commerce does not run on schedules, whereas it is nearly impossible to find a traditional store that is open 24/7. Websites are open all day long and clients can buy whatever they want whenever they want it.

3. Less costs: Not needing a physical store reduces the costs of running a traditional business. In addition, when e-commerce brings suppliers together with consumers there are not even production costs.

4. Bigger profit margin: Cost reduction and market extension mean that, even with lower prices, a bigger profit margin can be obtained than with a traditional store. More products are sold and more money is made.

5. Scalability: This means that you can sell to either one or to a thousand people at the same time. In a physical store there is always a limit to the number of clients that you can assist at the same time. On the other hand, with e-commerce, the only limit is your ability to attract clients.

E-commerce Does not Come with Only Advantages.

That is why it is also advisable to analyze the challenges that you will have to face when you begin your online adventure.

Disadvantages (Challenges)

- Lack of trust: Although payment platforms have evolved to the point of being as secure as any physical business, or even more so, a lot of people still think that less payment security, lack of trust. This means mistrust. We can help solve it by adding an SSL (https) certificate that encrypts the transferred information as well as by adding other stamps that transmit the necessary trust.

- Products and services that "cannot be seen or touched": Everyone likes the feeling of making a good investment. A way of making that feeling real is by seeing and touching the products with our hands. That tangible feeling is missing in an e-commerce shop. How can we solve it? With very thorough product cards and by adding images, videos, and very detailed descriptions of the products.

- Requiring access to the Internet: This is obvious, but to be able to buy and sell, you need a connected device. Nowadays, the large majority of people have this kind of access, but there are some sectors in which the target audience is either older or less "techy", which could be a problem.

- Technical problems: Any type of entrepreneurship, whether it is offline or on-line, implies dealing with unfamiliar issues. In the specific case of an e-commerce shop, the technological part requires a minimum knowledge that not everyone has. The best way to solve this is by outsourcing that part, although, of course, that carries a cost.

- Competitors: The initial investment in order to start an e-commerce is not as high as the initial cost of a physical business. This means more competitors.

- It takes time to get results: When a physical store is opened, the products are being shown to potential clients right from the very first minute. For an e-commerce, gaining visibility is more difficult than most people may think. You could have a great product and a great platform, but if you don't work on your visibility, nobody will see them.

Distribution Channel

Distribution channel refers to the network used to get a product from the manufacturer or creator to the end user.

When a distribution channel is "direct," the manufacturer is selling directly to the end user without a middleman. When the distribution channel is "indirect," the product changes hands several times before reaching the ultimate consumer. Intermediaries between the manufacturer and the consumer in an indirect distribution channel might include:

- Wholesaler/distributor
- Dealer
- Retailer
- Consultant
- Manufacturer's representative
- Catalog

There might be just one intermediary; there might be many.

Direct vs. Indirect Distribution Channels

A company that sells directly to consumers through direct mail, a catalog of its own products, or its own ecommerce site represents a business that uses a direct distribution channel. For example, entrepreneurs who create and sell digital products that include workbooks, audio training, and online courses from their own websites are using a direct distribution channel. The digital products go directly from the creator to the customer.

On a larger scale, the beverage alcohol industry uses a multi-tier, indirect distribution channel. Distillers and wineries sell to distributors, who sell to retailers, who sell to consumers. But while wineries must use indirect distribution channels to get their wines into retail outlets where consumers can buy them, many also sell directly to consumers onsite at wineries. Using both approaches lets wineries reach a mass market through an indirect distribution channel and a smaller market through direct distribution via on-site retail operations that they own.

Distribution Channel Considerations

Businesses with products should ask a number of questions before determining a distribution program. Those questions include:

- How does the end-user like to purchase these types of products? Does the consumer want to touch and examine the product or is it a product that the target audience likes to buy online?

- What, if any, are the local, regional, or national regulations regarding the product category's distribution channels?

- Does the customer need personalized service?

- Does the product itself need to be serviced?

- Does the product need to be installed?

- How is the product typically distributed and sold in your industry?

The distribution channel will have an impact on pricing. With indirect distribution, a product that goes from the manufacturer to a distributor before it goes to a retail outlet needs to be priced at wholesale so that both the distributor and retailer can mark up the price. With a multi-tier distribution channel, it looks like this:

- The manufacturer's customer is the distributor.

- The distributor's customer is the retailer.

- The retailer's customer is the consumer.

The manufacturer, distributor, and retailer all need to make money on that product.

The direct-to-consumer price is often the same as the price of a product that has been marked up several times through indirect distribution.

Billing Settlement Plan

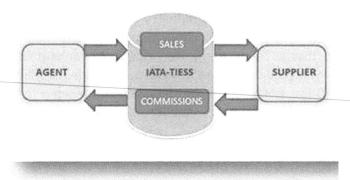

The billing and settlement plan (BSP) is a standardised system for airlines and agents, providing them with a simplified approach to the selling, reporting and administration of passenger air transportation. It is established under the general jurisdiction of the Passenger Agency Conference (PAConf), delegated to the BSP Committee (BSPC) and co-ordinated by the Agency Administrator/Plan Management.

Agents are able to:

- Issue neutral Standard Traffic Documents (STD) on behalf of all BSP Airlines, in accordance with their Sales Agency Agreements.

- Report with a minimum of effort, their sales made on behalf of BSP Airlines to a central EDP Centre, which produces one billing for each Agent's sales in a given period, requiring only one remittance per Agent and per period.

- Computes the division of the Agents' remittances to each BSP Airline, allowing one single settlement, within an agreed time frame.

Working of a BSP

Instead of every agent having an individual relationship with each airline, all of the information is consolidated through the BSP.

Agents make one single payment to the BSP (remittance), covering sales on all BSP Airlines. The BSP makes one consolidated payment to each airline, covering sales made by all agents in the country/region.

Agents are provided with a range of electronic ticket numbers to be used for sales on any airline.

Working Processes for Agents

1. Preparation to Sell on Behalf of Airlines

Before an agent can begin selling on behalf of airlines, the following must take place:

- A range of electronic ticket numbers are assigned to the Agent.

- The Airline assigns ticketing authority to the Agent to allow issue of ETs.

- Agents need to have access to an IATA-approved ticketing system such as a Global Distribution System (GDS).

2. Reporting by Agents

The agent reports all sales and refunds at the end of the reporting period. This is done electronically, through BSPlink. All transactions are forwarded to a central BSP Data Processing Centre (DPC).

3. Processing by BSP

The Data Processing Centre:

- Captures the tickets and refunds information from data files that have been transmitted by the GDS/ticketing system or other automated system such as BSPlink.

- Processes all relevant data and produce an "Agents Billing Analysis" for each agent. This analysis is compiled from the information of one or more reporting periods.

- Forwards a statement of sales made by Agents to each BSP Airline. This statement is compiled from the information of one or more reporting periods.

- Monitors ET ranges and provide replenishment as necessary.

4. Payment

The Agent makes just one net remittance covering all its BSP transactions for that period for all BSP Airlines. The BSP preferred method of payment is by direct debit.

5. Follow up by Airlines

The accounting department of each airline audits incoming data and addresses debit/credit accounting memoranda (ADM/ACM) to agents as necessary.

Benefits of the BSP

Simplification

The Agent is assured of a steady and pre-determined supply of neutral Standard Traffic Documents. The Agent uses the same Standard Traffic Documents on behalf of all BSP Airlines. The Agent issues one single sales report to one central point and effects one single remittance.

Savings

Training of Agents is simpler and shorter, due to one set of standard procedures. Centralisation of the processing and of the distribution of STDs reduces costs and allows for better control. Investigations by BSP Manager, who is empowered to take immediate action on behalf of BSP Airlines, allows for faster solutions to problems.

Control

The control system embodied in the BSP presents the following advantages: Billing and billing analyses of uniform presentation for Airlines and for Agents are rapidly produced by a neutral billing/collection agency. Airlines and Agents benefit from having the monitoring of Irregularity and Default effected by a neutral BSP Manager.

Automation Potential

Automation of back office functions is rendered by a single accounting system. BSP enables and encourages the use of the most modern automated ticket issuing devices, thereby economising in time and money, whilst presenting the customer with an attractive and legible ticket.

Digital Currency

Digital currency is also known as electronic money or digital money and differs from the physical currency that is banknotes and coins. The idea of digital currency is relatively new as it was proposed in 1983. Digital currencies possess attributes like those of physical currencies, but they enable real-time transactions as well as borderless transfer-of-ownership. Digital currencies can enable users to purchase products although others are only used in specific communities. Examples of digital currencies are cryptocurrencies. Digital currencies can be centralized where the money supply is controlled by one point of control or decentralized where several sources can supply the money.

Development of Digital Currencies

The concept of digital cash was first proposed by David Chaum in a research paper drafted in 1983. He subsequently established DigiCash in 1990 in Amsterdam which was an electronic cash firm intended on commercializing his concept. By 1998, the company had filed for bankruptcy and Chaum left it in 1999. Coca-Cola proposed buying from vending machines via mobile payments in 1997 and Paypal began operating in 1998. Another system called e-gold faced legal issues since it was used by criminals prompting the US Feds to raid it in 2005. The origins of digital currencies can be traced back to the dot-com boom of the 1990s. E-gold is recognized as one of the first as it began operating in 1996 and it was backed by gold. Another one was Liberty Reserve where users could exchange euros for dollars to Liberty Reserve Dollars or even Euros. The two services however gained a reputation of aiding money laundering and their operations were halted by the US. Q coins emerged in 2005 on the messaging platform Tencent QQ and became popular in China. Bitcoin, introduced in 2009, is extensively used and accepted and it is regarded as the first decentralized digital money.

Differences with Virtual and Traditional Currencies

The terms virtual and digital are mistakenly used interchangeably. Virtual currencies are a kind of digital currency, but the vice versa is incorrect. Virtual currencies are not used in the real world, but rather they are used on virtual platforms such as games. Most of the virtual currencies are centralized where the developers of the virtual world supply the currencies. Digital currencies, on the other hand, can be traded in exchange for physical products. Bitcoins and other cryptocurrencies are a kind of virtual currencies as they can replace cash. The bulk of the traditional money supply is held in banks on computer systems, and this is also regarded as digital currency. Although arguments may be raised that all currencies are becoming digital in the context of an increasingly cashless society, they are not declared to the public as such.

Types of Digital Currency

The following are 10 types of digital currencies and how they work:

1. Ethereum

Ethereum is a decentralized computing platform that features smart contract functionality. It offers the Ethereum Virtual Machine (EVM), a decentralized virtual machine that executes peer-to-peer contracts using a cryptocurrency known as ether. The Ethereum platform allows multiple uses concerning smart contracts. With Ethereum, you can safely do business with a person you don't know; because all terms are spelled out in a "smart contract" entrenched in the blockchain.

2. Ripple

Ripple is a real-time currency exchange, remittance network, and settlement system. It offers instant, certain, low-cost international payments. Also known as Ripple protocol or the Ripple Transaction Protocol (RTXP), it is built upon a decentralized open source Internet protocol and native currency referred to as XRP (ripples). Bases around public ledger, Ripple uses a consensus process to all exchange, remittance and payments in distributed process.

3. Litecoin

Litecoin is a peer-to-peer cryptocurrency released under the MIT/X11 license. The currency is inspired by and technically almost identical to bitcoin. Litecoin formation and transfer is based on an open source protocol.

4. Dash

Dash, formally called Darkcoin is a more secretive form of Bitcoin. It provides more privacy as it operates on a distributed mastercode network that makes dealings nearly untraceable. Launched in 2014, the currency has an increasing fan. Created and developed by Evan Duffield, this cryptocurrency according to Fernando Gutierrez from Dash.org, has X11 ASICs that presently mine Dash and CPU mining is not profitable anymore since a while ago.

5. Peercoin

Also known as PPCoin, Peercoin was created by software developers Scott Nadal and Sunny King. Lunched in 2012, it was the first digital currency to use a combination of proof-of-work and proof-of-stake. At first, the coins are mined using the proof-of-work hashing process. Over time, as the hashing difficulty increases, the users are rewarded coins using the proof-of-stake algorithm that requires minimal energy to generate blocks.

6. Dogecoin

Launched in 2013, Dogecoin is largely based on the Bitcoin protocol, but with some modifications. The currency uses the technology of scrypt as a proof-of-work scheme. Its block time is 60 seconds. There is no limit to the number of Dogecoin that can be produced. The digital currency deals with many coins that are lesser in value individually. Therefore, it has low entry barrier and good for carrying out smaller transactions.

7. Primecoin

Primecoin was developed by Sunny King. Its proof-of-work is built on prime numbers, and therefore, different from the common system of hashcash utilized by many cryptocurrencies built on the Bitcoin framework. The currency involves finding distinctive long chains of prime numbers and provides greater mining ease and security to the network.

8. Chinacoin

Chinacoin is a litecoin-based digital currency that uses the scrypt password-based key derivation function. At the moment, it is generated in 60-second blocks with an about 88 coins per block.

9. Ven

Ven is a global digital currency that is designed to allow trade among members of Hub Culture. Launched in 2007, Ven is aimed at reducing the risk of inflation. The Ven value is determined on the financial markets from a basket of commodities, currencies and carbon futures.

10. Bitcoin

Bitcoin is a digital currency created by the mysterious Satoshi Nakamoto. Like other currencies, bitcoin can be used to buy items locally and electronically. As a new user, you can use Bitcoin without understanding all its technical details. Once you install a Bitcoin wallet on your mobile phone or computer, it will generate the first Bitcoin address and you can generate more whenever you need them. After creating bitcoins, you can use them for all types of real transactions.

Adoption By Governments

More than 24 nations had invested in distributed ledger technologies by 2016. Hong Kong introduced the Octopus card system in 1997 which allows public transport users to use a contactless smart card. The system enjoyed rapid popularity and is now widely used to pay for public transport in Hong Kong. Some merchants also accept the Octopus Card. The success of the Octopus Card facilitated the development of the Oyster

Card in London. Residents of London use the card to access transportation in the tube, buses, trams, London Overground and most of the City's National Rail Service. Zug in Switzerland has made strides towards adopting digital currencies. The municipality included bitcoins as a method of paying little amounts to a maximum of 200 SFr. Zug promptly converts the bitcoins accepted into the country's currency. Other countries have either proposed or are working on introducing digital currencies. The Bank of Canada, for example, has assembled partners and experts in trying to create its currency's version on the blockchain. Netherlands' central bank has been doing trial runs for a virtual currency based on Bitcoin referred to as "DNBCoin."

Cryptocurrency

A cryptocurrency is a digital or virtual currency designed to work as a medium of exchange. It uses cryptography to secure and verify transactions as well as to control the creation of new units of a particular cryptocurrency. Essentially, cryptocurrencies are limited entries in a database that no one can change unless specific conditions are fulfilled.

There have been many attempts at creating a digital currency during the 90s tech boom, with systems like Flooz, Beenz and DigiCash emerging on the market but inevitably failing. There were many different reasons for their failures, such as fraud, financial problems and even frictions between companies' employees and their bosses.

Notably, all of those systems utilized a Trusted Third Party approach, meaning that the companies behind them verified and facilitated the transactions. Due to the failures of these companies, the creation of a digital cash system was seen as a lost cause for a long while.

Then, in early 2009, an anonymous programmer or a group of programmers under an alias Satoshi Nakamoto introduced Bitcoin. Satoshi described it as a 'peer-to-peer electronic cash system.' It is completely decentralized, meaning there are no servers involved and no central controlling authority. The concept closely resembles peer-to-peer networks for file sharing.

One of the most important problems that any payment network has to solve is double-spending. It is a fraudulent technique of spending the same amount twice. The traditional solution was a trusted third party - a central server - that kept records of the balances and transactions. However, this method always entailed an authority basically in control of your funds and with all your personal details on hand.

In a decentralized network like Bitcoin, every single participant needs to do this job. This is done via the Blockchain - a public ledger of all transaction that ever happened within the network, available to everyone. Therefore, everyone in the network can see every account's balance.

Every transaction is a file that consists of the sender's and recipient's public keys (wallet addresses) and the amount of coins transferred. The transaction also needs to be signed off by the sender with their private key. All of this is just basic cryptography. Eventually, the transaction is broadcasted in the network, but it needs to be confirmed first.

Within a cryptocurrency network, only miners can confirm transactions by solving a cryptographic puzzle. They take transactions, mark them as legitimate and spread them across the network. Afterwards, every node of the network adds it to its database. Once the transaction is confirmed it becomes unforgeable and irreversible and a miner receives a reward, plus the transaction fees.

Essentially, any cryptocurrency network is based on the absolute consensus of all the participants regarding the legitimacy of balances and transactions. If nodes of the network disagree on a single balance, the system would basically break. However, there are a lot of rules pre-built and programmed into the network that prevents this from happening.

Cryptocurrencies are so called because the consensus-keeping process is ensured with strong cryptography. This, along with aforementioned factors, makes third parties and blind trust as a concept completely redundant.

Uses of Cryptocurrency

Buy Goods

In the past, trying to find a merchant that accepts cryptocurrency was extremely difficult, if not impossible. These days, however, the situation is completely different.

There are a lot of merchants - both online and offline - that accept Bitcoin as the form of payment. They range from massive online retailers like Overstock and Newegg to small local shops, bars and restaurants. Bitcoins can be used to pay for hotels, flights, jewelery, apps, computer parts and even a college degree.

Other digital currencies like Litecoin, Ripple, Ethereum and so on aren't accepted as widely just yet. Things are changing for the better though, with Apple having authorized at least 10 different cryptocurrencies as a viable form of payment on App Store.

Of course, users of cryptocurrencies other than Bitcoin can always exchange their coins for BTCs. Moreover, there are Gift Card selling websites like Gift Off, which accepts around 20 different cryptocurrencies. Through gift cards, you can essentially buy anything with a cryptocurrency.

Finally, there are marketplaces like Bitify and OpenBazaar that only accept cryptocurrencies.

Invest

Many people believe that cryptocurrencies are the hottest investment opportunity currently available. Indeed, there are many stories of people becoming millionaires through their Bitcoin investments. Bitcoin is the most recognizable digital currency to date, and just last year one BTC was valued at $800. In November 2017, the price of one Bitcoin exceeded $7,000.

Ethereum, perhaps the second most valued cryptocurrency, has recorded the fastest rise a digital currency ever demonstrated. Since May 2016, its value increased by at least 2,700 percent. When it comes to all cryptocurrencies combined, their market cap soared by more than 10,000 percent since mid-2013.

However, it is worth noting that cryptocurrencies are high-risk investments. Their market value fluctuates like no other asset's. Moreover, it is partly unregulated, there is always a risk of them getting outlawed in certain jurisdictions and any cryptocurrency exchange can potentially get hacked.

If you decide to invest in cryptocurrencies, Bitcoin is obviously still the dominant one. However, in 2017 its share in the crypto-market has quite dramatically fallen from 90 percent to just 40 percent. There are many options currently available, with some coins being privacy-focused, others being less open and decentralized than Bitcoin and some just outright copying it.

While it's very easy to buy Bitcoins - there are numerous exchanges in existence that trade in BTC - other cryptocurrencies aren't as easy to acquire. Although, this situation is slowly improving with major exchanges like Kraken, BitFinex, BitStamp and many others starting to sell Litecoin, Ethereum, Monero, Ripple and so on. There are also a few other different ways of being coin, for instance, you can trade face-to-face with a seller or use a Bitcoin ATM.

Once you bought your cryptocurrency, you need a way to store it. All major exchanges offer wallet services. But, while it might seem convenient, it's best if you store your assets in an offline wallet on your hard drive, or even invest in a hardware wallet. This is the most secure way of storing your coins and it gives you full control over your assets.

As with any other investment, you need to pay close attention to the cryptocurrencies' market value and to any news related to them. Coinmarketcap is a one-stop solution for tracking the price, volume, circulation supply and market cap of most existing cryptocurrencies.

Depending on a jurisdiction you live in, once you've made a profit or a loss investing in cryptocurrencies, you might need to include it in your tax report. In terms of taxation, cryptocurrencies are treated very differently from country to country. In the US, the Internal Revenue Service ruled that Bitcoins and other digital currencies are to be taxed as property, not currency. For investors, this means that accrued long-term gains and losses from cryptocurrency trading are taxed at each investor's applicable capital gains rate, which stands at a maximum of 15 percent.

Mine

Miners are the single most important part of any cryptocurrency network, and much like trading, mining is an investment. Essentially, miners are providing a bookkeeping service for their respective communities. They contribute their computing power to solving complicated cryptographic puzzles, which is necessary to confirm a transaction and record it in a distributed public ledger called the Blockchain.

One of the interesting things about mining is that the difficulty of the puzzles is constantly increasing, correlating with the number of people trying to solve it. So, the more popular a certain cryptocurrency becomes, the more people try to mine it, the more difficult the process becomes.

A lot of people have made fortunes by mining Bitcoins. Back in the days, you could make substantial profits from mining using just your computer, or even a powerful enough laptop. These days, Bitcoin mining can only become profitable if you're willing to invest in an industrial-grade mining hardware. This, of course, incurs huge electricity bills on top of the price of all the necessary equipment.

Currently, Litecoins, Dogecoins and Feathercoins are said to be the best cryptocurrencies in terms of being cost-effective for beginners. For instance, at the current value of Litecoins, you might earn anything from 50 cents to 10 dollars a day using only consumer-grade hardware.

But how do miners make profits? The more computing power they manage to accumulate, the more chances they have of solving the cryptographic puzzles. Once a miner manages to solve the puzzle, they receive a reward as well as a transaction fee.

As a cryptocurrency attracts more interest, mining becomes harder and the amount of coins received as a reward decreases. For example, when Bitcoin was first created, the reward for successful mining was 50 BTC. Now, the reward stands at 12.5 Bitcoins. This happened because the Bitcoin network is designed so that there can only be a total of 21 mln coins in circulation.

As of November 2017, almost 17 mln Bitcoins have been mined and distributed. However, as rewards are going to become smaller and smaller, every single Bitcoin mined will become exponentially more and more valuable.

All of those factors make mining cryptocurrencies an extremely competitive arms race that rewards early adopters. However, depending on where you live, profits made from mining can be subject to taxation and Money Transmitting regulations. In the US, the FinCEN has issued a guidance, according to which mining of cryptocurrencies and exchanging them for flat currencies may be considered money transmitting. This means that miners might need to comply with special laws and regulations dealing with this type of activities.

Accept as Payment (For Business)

If you happen to own a business and if you're looking for potential new customers, accepting cryptocurrencies as a form of payment may be a solution for you. The interest in cryptocurrencies has never been higher and it's only going to increase. Along with the growing interest, also grows the number of crypto-ATMs located around the world. Coin ATM Radar currently lists almost 1,800 ATMs in 58 countries.

First of all, you need to let your customers know that your business accepts crypto coins. Simply putting a sign by your cash register should do the trick. The payments can then be accepted using hardware terminals, touch screen apps or simple wallet addresses through QR codes.

There are many different services that you can use to be able to accept payments in cryptocurrencies. For example, CoinPayments currently accepts over 75 different digital currencies, charging just 0.5 percent commission per transaction. Other popular services include Cryptonator, CoinGate and BitPay, with the latter only accepting Bitcoins.

In the US, Bitcoin and other cryptocurrencies have been recognized as a convertible virtual currency, which means accepting them as a form of payment is exactly the same as accepting cash, gold or gift cards.

For tax purposes, US-based businesses accepting cryptocurrencies need to record a reference of sales, amount received in a particular currency and the date of transaction. If sales taxes are payable, the amount due is calculated based on the average exchange rate at the time of sale.

Legality of Cryptocurrencies

As cryptocurrencies are becoming more and more mainstream, law enforcement agencies, tax authorities and legal regulators worldwide are trying to understand the very concept of crypto coins and where exactly do they fit in existing regulations and legal frameworks.

With the introduction of Bitcoin, the first ever cryptocurrency, a completely new paradigm was created. Decentralized, self-sustained digital currencies that don't exist in any physical shape or form and are not controlled by any singular entity were always set to cause an uproar among the regulators.

A lot of concerns have been raised regarding cryptocurrencies' decentralized nature and their ability to be used almost completely anonymously. The authorities all over the world are worried about the cryptocurrencies' appeal to the traders of illegal goods and services. Moreover, they are worried about their use in money laundering and tax evasion schemes.

As of November 2017, Bitcoin and other digital currencies are outlawed only in Bangladesh, Bolivia, Ecuador, Kyrgyzstan and Vietnam, with China and Russia being on the verge of banning them as well. Other jurisdictions, however, do not make the usage of cryptocurrencies illegal as of yet, but the laws and regulations can vary drastically depending on the country.

Storing Cryptocurrencies

Unlike most traditional currencies, cryptocurrencies are digital, which entails a completely different approach, particularly when it comes to storing it. Technically, you don't store your units of cryptocurrency; instead it's the private key that you use to sign for transactions that need to be securely stored.

There are several different types of cryptocurrency wallets that cater for different needs. If your priority is privacy, you might want to opt for a paper or a hardware wallet. Those are the most secure ways of storing your crypto funds. There are also 'cold' (offline) wallets that are stored on your hard drive and online wallets, which can either be affiliated with exchanges or with independent platforms.

Buying Cryptocurrencies

There are a lot of different options when it comes to buying Bitcoins. For example, there are currently almost 1,800 Bitcoin ATMs in 58 countries. Moreover, you can buy BTC using gift cards, cryptocurrency exchanges, investment trusts and you can even trade face-to-face.

When it comes to other, less popular cryptocurrencies, the buying options aren't as diverse. However, there are still numerous exchanges where you can acquire various crypto-coins for flat currencies or Bitcoins. Face-to-face trading is also a popular way of acquiring coins. Buying options depend on particular cryptocurrencies, their popularity as well as your location.

Electronic Trading

Electronic stock trading, or E-trading, is the practice of buying and selling stock and other assets using an electronic stock brokerage service. Electronic trading services allow users to sign up over the Internet and conduct stock transactions using a purely electronic interface on the Web.

Electronic trading is easy: Log in to your account. Select the security you wish to buy or sell. Click the mouse or tap your screen, and the transaction takes place. From an investor's perspective, it's simple and easy. But behind the scenes, it is a complex process backed by an impressive array of technology. What was once associated with shouting traders and wild hand gestures has now become more closely associated with statisticians and computer programmers.

First Step: Open an Account

The first step is to open an account with a brokerage firm. This can be done electronically or by completing and mailing the appropriate forms. You will need to provide personal information, such as your name and address that enables the firm to identify you, along with a bit of information about your investing experience level. Then the brokerage firm can evaluate whether the account you are seeking is appropriate. For example, if you have no experience trading stocks but wish to open an account that lets you trade using borrowed money (a margin account), your application may be denied.

The account-opening process also enables you to designate electronic pathways between your bank account and brokerage account so that money can move in either direction. Should you wish to add more money to your investable pool, you can move it from your bank account to your brokerage account simply by logging in to your account. Similarly, if your investments have generated gains and you need that money to pay bills, you can move from your brokerage account to your bank without making any phone calls. If you don't have a bank account, you can set up a money market account with the brokerage firm and use it in a manner similar to a bank account.

These electronic conveniences require computer equipment, such as servers, and human oversight to make sure everything is set up properly and works as planned. The technological requirements become even more complex when you are ready to trade.

Working

Before you place an order, you will likely want to learn about the security you are considering for purchase. Most brokerage websites offer access to research reports that will help you make your decision, and real-time quotes that tell how much the security is trading for at any given time. The research reports are updated periodically and loaded to the website when you access them. The quotes are a far more complex issue, as the technology must keep track of thousands of data points relating to stock prices and deliver that data to you instantly upon request.

When you actually place an order, the infrastructure level required to support the process increases again. Programming and technology must facilitate order entry and the variety of choices that it entails. First, you have the option to select your choice of order types. Market orders execute immediately. Limit orders can be set to execute only at a certain price, within a certain time limit ranging from immediately to anytime within a period of months. These choices are available simultaneously to all investors using the system and must work in real time.

The purchase price and share quantity requested must be conveyed to the marketplace, which requires the computer system at the brokerage firm where the order was placed to interact with computer systems on the securities exchange where the shares will be purchased. The systems at the exchange must instantly and simultaneously interact with the systems at all of the brokerage firms, either offering shares for sale or seeking to purchase shares.

To complicate matters further, the electronic interface must include all exchanges (Nasdaq, NYSE, etc.) from which an investor may choose to purchase a security. The interaction between systems must execute transactions and deliver the best price for the trade. To prove to regulators like the Securities and Exchange Commission (SEC) that the trade was executed in a timely and cost-effective fashion, the systems must maintain a record of the transaction.

The computerized matching engine must perform a high volume of transactions every minute the market is open for business and do so instantly and flawlessly. Backup systems are necessary to make sure investors have access to their accounts and can trade every minute the markets are open. Security industry regulators, such as the SEC, also need access to the information contained in investors' accounts.

That data is held at the Depository Trust Company, which is a recordkeeper responsible for maintaining details for all shareholders in the United States. The DTCC is a holding companyconsisting of five clearing corporations and one depository, making it the world's largest financial services corporation dealing in post-trade transactions. This central repository serves as a backstop, enabling investors to recover account information in the event the brokerage firm responsible for facilitating the investor's trades goes out of business.

Once the trade has been made, the transaction must be confirmed with both buyer and seller. The data must be sent back out to the systems that collect and display pricing to other market participants to facilitate trading in the broader marketplace.

A record of the transaction must be stored, so that data is available for client statements and for clients to access online when they log into their brokerage accounts. On an ongoing basis the system must capture data for corporate actions like dividends and capital gains, not only to keep the investor's account balance up to date and accurate but also to facilitate tax reporting. Enormous volumes of data must continually be tracked, captured and transmitted.

The system must also be able to facilitate both periodic and regularly scheduled recurring transactions. Everything from transfers to and from the investor's personal bank account to ongoing transfers between accounts for account funding, bill payment, estate settlement and a variety of other transactions must be supported.

Risks

Electronic trading is integral to the financial markets. Everything from technological glitches to outright fraud can impair the smooth and efficient functioning of those markets, costing brokerage firms money and calling into question the credibility of the financial system. Even minor glitches, such as the "flash crash" of May 6, 2010, can wreak havoc. The flash crash was a brief trading glitch that caused the Dow Jones Industrial Average to plunge 998.5 points in just 20 minutes. More than $1 trillion in market value disappeared. To rectify the situation and make investors whole, 21,000 trades were canceled—all because of a single glitch, triggered by an order placed in the futures market on a brokerage firm's computer system, which caused panic trading to spill over to the equity markets.

Advantages of E-trading

Electronic stock trading can have several advantages over traditional trading through a live broker.

Ease of Access

One benefit of online stock trading services is that they are easy for anyone to access and use. All that is required to use most online trading services is an Internet connection and funds in a checking account to invest. Accounts can often be set up within a few days and transfers can be made into accounts from a linked checking account on demand, so you can get money into investments quickly if necessary.

Cost

Another potential advantage of electronic trading is that the cost of transactions can be much less than using a traditional stock broker. Flesh and blood stock brokers are highly trained professionals; when you place a trade with real stock brokers you pay a premium for their time. Electronic trading services are automated, which can reduce the cost of placing trades, allowing electronic services to charge low transaction fees. For instance, Sharebuilder, a popular online trading service, charges $4 per investment when buying shares of a specific stock or mutual fund using their automatic investing tools.

Self-Directed Investing

Many investors pay investment professionals to manage their investments for them. While this can have advantages for those who do not understand investing, professional services often charge commissions that can sap investment gains. Electronic investing allows users to direct their own investments and buy and sell whenever they please without having to interact with middlemen.

Convenience

Electronic stock trading also offers greater convenience than using a conventional stock broker. With online trading, trades can be made anywhere as long as you have access to the internet. For instance, if you are on a business trip to China, you could make trades from a laptop at your hotel without having to call anyone. Accounts are typically accessible at any time of the day, allowing users to look over their investments whenever they please.

Subscription Levels

Electronic stock trading services may offer a variety of subscription levels for different types of investors. For instance, some accounts are free and charge fees only when you make trades. Others may charge monthly fees, but allow traders to make trades for less money, which can be advantageous to investors that expect to trade often.

Electronic Ticket

An electronic ticket or E-ticket replaces paper tickets with passenger name, itinerary, date and price on it. Instead of being printed on the ticket, this information is stored in a Luxair data base, after the booking and payment have been effected.

Working

After we have received your e-mail confirming your reservation and after the payment has been effected per credit card, you will get a copy of the itinerary containing the following information:

- Name and first name of the passenger
- E-ticket number

- – Reservation number

- – Flight number; date; destinations; departure and

- – Arrival time

- – Price

- – Extracts of the Warsaw Convention

Reading an E-ticket (Airplane)

E-ticket receipts can be tricky to decipher – there's a bunch of hieroglyphics (aka travel-speak) on any given one.

That said, there's some very basic and important information there, specifically: date and city info, your airline and flight numbers and also the electronic ticket number, which is important to have if you're looking to retroactively access your file (to add frequent flyer info or to attempt a post-date refund, for example).

Otherwise, here's how to read an e ticket:

A – validating carrier
B – means that this document can't be used to board your flight
C – place and date of issue
D – electronic ticket number
E – passenger name
F – departure airport code
G – arrival airport codes
H – airline code and flight numbers
I – class of service and travel dates

Ways to use E-tickets

Travelers can get e-tickets in a number of ways. They can contact a travel agency, which can make the arrangements. They also can contact the airline directly or use an online site.

Travelers must provide standard biographical and ticketing information, such as name and address, phone number and e-mail addresses, as well as destination and travel dates. In most cases, a credit or debit card is required for the actual purchase.

The seller or agency sends an e-mail to the purchaser's account, confirming the purchase and details of the trip. Sometimes they will send them the e-ticket (which the buyer can print) and sometimes they will send a link to an airline Web site, where the passenger can view or download the e-ticket and travel itinerary. It is a good practice to save these e-mails and print them out, as it can help confirm the ticket purchase in the event of a problem.

Some online e-ticketing services will save a traveler's flight information online, enabling that person to access it at any time from different locations simply by logging on to the site and entering a password. Printing this out will suffice as a paper receipt.

Airport security procedures usually call for e-ticket flyers to present government-issued photo identification to claim their ticket and receive a boarding pass. (International travelers: Don't forget your passport and/or visa.) In some cases, other documents or the credit/debit card used to make the online purchase may be required. Passengers should check with individual airlines for appropriate documentation requirements. It is recommended that passengers arrive and check in at the airport -- either at the airline counter or a self-serve kiosk, if available -- at least one hour prior to your flight. This allows time to iron out any last-minute issues. However, some e-ticket holders can check in for their flight from their home computer.

Once passengers satisfy these requirements, the airline issues a boarding pass, which will allow them through other security checkpoints and onto the aircraft.

The Future of E-Tickets

It is safe to say airline e-tickets are here to stay. They already make up a majority of the market, and the industry is committed to increasing that percentage. Airlines are moving toward a "self-service model," with passengers researching, booking, buying, checking in and boarding virtually without airline assistance.

As all this occurs, analysts foresee great improvements in standardizing e-ticketing among airlines. Continental Airlines, for example, this year announced it had implemented a standardized system with 77 carriers both domestic and internationally, allowing passengers to travel on any of them using a single, paperless e-tickets.

The industry also plans continued improvements in flexibility, reliability and real-time updates. Some of this will depend upon other advancements in Internet software and hardware advances, as well as improvements in wireless technology. The airlines, for instance, are working on plans to increase the number of multi-carrier self-serve kiosks at major airports. The industry also wants to adopt a standardized bar coding system to increase the speed and accuracy of check-in and boarding passes.

The public's comfort level with e-business transactions -- online bill paying, shopping and such -- is rising. Some hotels also are installing self-serve airline e-ticket kiosks in their lobbies, where travelers can make plans and receive updates on their flights. At the same time, some airlines already are charging passengers up to $20 for the "extra" service of providing them with a paper ticket. With these and other factors looming, there are many reasons to believe the paper ticket will be totally replaced by its electronic cousin, the e-ticket.

References

- E-commerce: searchcio.techtarget.com, Retrieved 10 March 2018

- What-is-an-e-ticket: airtreks.com, Retrieved 16 June 2018

- What-is-e-commerce: doofinder.com, Retrieved 04 August 2018

- 10-types-digital-currencies-work: techbullion.com, Retrieved 19 March 2018

- Basics-mechanics-behind-electronic-trading-110713: investopedia.com, Retrieved 10 May 2018

- Benefits-electronic-trading-6694466: pocketsense.com, Retrieved 14 June 2018

- What-is-a-digital-currency: worldatlas.com, Retrieved 26 July 2018

Permissions

Index

CPSIA information can be obtained
at www.ICGtesting.com
Printed in the USA
BVHW011515060619
550362BV00003B/305/P